My Road to Québec

Canadian Cataloguing In Publication Data

Charest, Jean, 1958-

Jean Charest: my Road to Québec

Autobiography.
Issued also in French under title: Jean Charest.

ISBN 2-89051-722-5

1. Charest, Jean, 1958- . 2. Quebec Liberal Party.
3. Quebec (Province) – Politics and government • 1994 .
4. Progressive Conservative Party of Canada. 5. Canada •
Politics and government – 1993- . 6. Politicians • Quebec
(Province) – Biography. 7. Politicians • Canada – Biography.
I. Title.

FC2926.1.C45A313 1998   971.4'04'092   C98-941607-0
F1053.2.25.C45A313 1998

Cover photography: Éric Lajeunesse
Back cover photography: Grant Siméon
Typesetting: Infographie DN

Legal deposit : 4th trimester 1998
National Library of Canada
National Library of Québec

123456789 IG 98

Copyright © Ottawa, Canada, 1998
Éditions Pierre Tisseyre
ISBN 2-89051-722-5
10892

Jean Charest

My Road to Québec

ÉDITIONS
PIERRE TISSEYRE

5757, Cypihot Street, Saint-Laurent (Québec) H4S 1R3
Telephone: (514) 334-2690 – Fax: (514) 334-8395
http://ed.tisseyre.qc.ca
E mail: info@ed.tisseyre.qc.ca

To Michou, Amélie,
Antoine and Alexandra,
I love you.

FOREWORD

On March 2nd, 1998, my life changed forever. Daniel Johnson announced he was stepping down from the leadership of the Québec Liberal Party. Within minutes, I began receiving calls at my office from Québec and all over the country urging me to succeed him, despite the fact that I was the leader of a federal party. For almost fourteen years I represented the people of Sherbrooke in Parliament. I loved my work because I care about the community I come from in the Eastern Townships. It is where I have spent most of my life. Québec is where I was born and where I grew up. To me, commitment to the people you represent must come before commitment to any one political party. Now I have come home, because I want to help build the kind of Québec we can be proud of handing down to our children.

The people of Sherbrooke know me well, and I have the privilege of knowing them. But I am less well known to Québecers from other regions, which led to the idea of writing this book. My friends suggested it mainly because they were being asked what kind of person I was and where I stood on different issues. That is why I decided to speak directly to Québecers and other Canadians about the values I grew up with, the beliefs I hold, the lessons my life in politics has taught me, and the reasons for the choices I have made.

We are headed into an election that will have a major impact on our collective future. I am writing this book with the hope of making Québec voters better informed about the choices before them, and because all Canadians need to know what they can do to help us build a better country.

Jean Charest
North Hatley, Québec, July-August 1998

Where I Come From

I was born in Sherbrooke, Québec, on the 24th of June, Saint Jean Baptiste Day, 1958. Here in the Townships is where I grew up. My mother, Rita Leonard, was from an Irish Catholic family. She came from a little village called Bury, close to the town of Sherbrooke. She wasn't a city person. She came from the country. Her father was a wood merchant and her family had emigrated to Canada during one of the famines that virtually depopulated Ireland during the nineteenth century. They had come in one of those coffin ships, where people were crammed together and locked up in the hold in the most appallingly unsanitary conditions for the thirty days it took to cross the Atlantic Ocean. Countless men, women and children died on those ships of hunger and disease. Their sufferings are almost unimaginable. To get a sense of the hardships they faced, you need only visit Grosse Île, the island on the St. Lawrence River where the survivors were quarantined on arrival. Some of those immigrants, who scattered all over North America, settled in the Eastern Townships. So, my mother grew up in an English-speaking family amid a wider community where the majority of the people were French-speaking. She and her five brothers and sisters learned to speak French when they were very young. My

mother attended the Collège Mont-Notre-Dame in Sherbrooke. In those days it had an English section, as did Villa
Maria and Sacred Heart Convent in Montreal.

My parents met when my mother was studying to
become a nurse and preparing to enter the job market.
My father was older than she was. The Charests on my
father's side have lived in Sherbrooke for several generations. Their ancestors were among the earliest settlers
of New France. They were merchants, business people. My
great-grandfather, Joe Charest, was an entrepreneur in
Sherbrooke. He owned several lumber camps in Québec
and the United States. My grandfather, Ludovic, was also a
business man. His company did land-clearing in northern
Québec and northern Ontario for hydro-electric companies. Later he did some work for Hydro-Québec and
Ontario Hydro. My father, meanwhile, became a hockey
player. His once successful family had fallen on hard times
during the Depression. My grandfather had taken some
big losses and was forced to start over with next to nothing.
My father's childhood was anything but golden. Hockey
was what got him through those difficult times. He was a
good player. During the Second World War he played for a
team in Saint-Paul-L'Ermite. Later he spent a season in the
American League.

By the time my parents met, my father had put an
end to his hockey-playing career. He bought a hotel called
the Manoir Orford, in Eastman. It became a popular
week-end meeting place for people who lived in Sherbrooke, Magog and the surrounding area. On week-ends it
attracted a lot of young people. Because of its location on
the road to Montreal, people would stop in on their way to
and from the city. My father owned it until 1958.

My parents were married in 1953. They had five
children. I was their third. That year my father sold the
hotel, purchased a house in Sherbrooke and went into
business. He dealt in real estate, but he also owned several

launderettes. Self-reliant, never having completed high-school, he was what you would call a self-made man.

We grew up in an environment where our mother spoke English, our father spoke French, and both were impeccably bilingual. We lived in the north end of Sherbrooke with many other families like ours where both languages were spoken. We learned young that all around us, in the society at large, there was something called diversity, and that diversity was something we were supposed to respect. That environment brought an added dimension to our lives. It enriched us by making us understand that things look a little different, and feel a little different, depending on the language you speak and the cultural background you happen to come from. We learned to feel at ease in either group and to move effortlessly between the two. Our parents stressed the importance of respecting and understanding others, of accepting different points of view, and realizing that there were many ways of viewing the world.

If the truth be known, my childhood was very blessed. I loved and admired my mother. She was brought up with a love of books, music, dance and poetry; she had an artistic side to her nature. My mother was a very articulate woman who had lived a rather hard life. She bore five children one after the other. She suffered from psoriasis, a chronic skin disease. I vividly remember that after the birth of her youngest child her body was covered with it. Life for her was very exacting. As children we demanded a lot from her; I realize that now. We were not exactly tame. I, for one, must have been a handful. At five I was so restless that I was sent to school a year early. The school, right near our home, was run by the Soeurs Jésus-Marie.

Another thing I remember from my childhood was the close proximity in which we lived to our maternal grand-parents, the Leonards. We shared the same back-yard. My grandmother Leonard had a green thumb. She had a beautiful garden where she grew all kinds of flowers. She was a gentle soul and a devout Catholic, like my mother, with whom she shared a deep religious faith. My mother was of a generation of women for whom there was no question as to what they were going to do with their lives. Her life was centered on her children and everything we undertook and strove for. She lived only for us.

My father believed strongly in self-reliance. In our house, *responsibility* was a word we often heard. We were responsible for our actions; we were expected to face up to the consequences of whatever we did. We learned very young that our future was in our own, not someone else's hands; that once we made a decision, we had to live with it. Our father felt so strongly about this that, one day, he came up with the idea that my brother Robert and I (we were respectively ten and nine at the time) should buy some peanut-vending machines for the purpose of installing them in his Laundromats. He arranged for us to go to the local Caisse Populaire to talk to the manager about taking out a loan. I can still see us now: Mr. Champagne, eyeing us from behind his big desk, asking what he could do for us, and my brother and me absolutely convinced that we were the ones contracting the loan. How he kept a straight face, I will never know. My father had told us, "You are going to borrow the money to buy the machines, and with the money you make from the peanuts you will repay part of the loan every month. You are going to draw up a budget. A percentage of your earnings will go to paying down the loan, another percentage will go to purchasing the peanuts, and whatever is left over will go into your pockets as profit."

That said, we had the last laugh. In our home all the children had chores assigned to them. My brother and I were in charge of shoveling the driveway and making a fire in the fireplace every day after school. Those were things you had to do without fail. In the summertime we were responsible for maintenance around the house, for cleaning the windows, and washing the kitchen floor. Each one of us had tasks to carry out. We were a fairly regimented household. So my father did his arithmetic. He paid my brother and me three dollars a week each, and I seem to remember that a crate of peanuts cost $5.60. He offered to transport the peanuts and to set our salary at one crate of peanuts (which he would buy on our behalf) per week. Then, very suddenly, the peanut market went crazy. Prices went through the roof—up to $9 a crate in the space of six months. Naturally my father tried to renegotiate our agreement. "Never!" we cried. "Never! A deal is a deal! Too bad!" I don't have to tell you that he was not amused. Whenever we went to the Caisse Populaire, the Cashiers always knew us because they would see a little hand appear on the counter clutching a very salty roll of five-cent pieces (learning to "roll" our money was just one of the many things we learned in the peanut business). For a couple of nine and ten year olds, it was quite an adventure.

In our house, as soon as we reached adolescence, we were expected to buy our own clothes and to go out and earn whatever pocket money we needed. The principle my father applied, and which he still lives by, was the following: As a business man he had good years when he made money, and other years when he earned less. He would always say to us, "I have one standard of living. That's how I live. I am very happy. I have enough to live on. Some years I make more, fine, I reinvest. Some years I earn a little less, but it doesn't affect me. I still have enough to get by." Nevertheless, it was very clear to us that material possessions did not count for everything in life.

My mother had a profound influence on the choices I was to make later on. Whenever we discussed my future, she would say, "one day, when you are old, you will want to take stock, to ask yourself what meaning you gave to your life. I can give you some clues as to the kind of answers you

are going to find. First, you are not going to find it by
counting the number of cars in your driveway. Nor will the
answer be determined by the size of your house or the
amount in your bank account. Some day the time will
come for you to ask yourself what you have done with your
life. That is why it is important, starting right now, to give
your life meaning." Maybe it was her unshakable faith that
made her say that, but she truly believed it.

In our family, the work ethic was front and center. My
father used to say, " In life there are three things you have
to do in order to succeed: The first is work. The second is
work. And the third is work." That was not some sort of
narrow, materialistic statement on his part, far from it. In
saying that, he meant that in everything you undertake, be
it your studies, your marriage, your relations with your
family or your career, you have to work at making those
things a success. He used to work seven days a week and,
on Sunday mornings, would often take us with him to the
office. On his desk, under glass, he kept a cartoon. He
would draw our attention to it almost every time we went
there. In the first panel it showed a boy with a net in his
hand chasing after a butterfly. The next panel had the boy
falling into a river because he had not been looking where
he was going. The last one showed the same boy clam-
bering out of the river still holding on to his net, which
now had a fish in it. He would point to the cartoon and
say, "You see the meaning of that. It means that in life, if
you work hard, you may not get what you were hoping for,
but you'll always get something. If you work hard, you
don't have to worry, you can't go wrong." For him, work
was a paramount value. You had to work hard, and you
had to put your heart into it. Equally important was self-
reliance. You had to be self-sufficient, look after your own
affairs, and you must not depend on others.

At the time, Québec society was undergoing major
changes. Separations and divorces were becoming more

common. Those things used to come up in family discussions around the dinner table. We had friends at school
and knew families in our neighbourhood who were experiencing the repercussions of these changes. It was new, and
it intrigued us. My father's approach was very straightforward. He told my sisters they had to arrange their lives
so as not to have to depend on anyone for their livelihood.
"Economically speaking, make sure you manage your own
affairs so that you can be independent."

Loyalty was also very important. You had to stand up
for yourself and defend your beliefs and your friends, even
when circumstances did not encourage you to do so. It was
presented to us as a test of our mettle and character. My
mother, being very devout, was more fatalistic than my
father, more resigned, as the Irish are often prone to be.
Later on in life I recognized many traits in my mother's
character that seemed to come from her Irish background. Certain cultural traits seem to be passed on from
generation to generation. Fatalism, resignation. Even if
you were struck down by some terrible misfortune, you
had to accept it, but you had to pick yourself up. In fact,
the other belief my parents held strongly was that if you
stumbled, that was all right, that happened in life, you
should not let it alarm you, you shouldn't be afraid of
failure. What really mattered was to get back on your feet.
"Life goes on," my mother would say. It is what I found
myself saying to my own daughter the day after the 1993
Tory leadership convention. After I said it, I suddenly
realized it was exactly what my mother would have said.
Amélie was very disappointed. She was ten years old and
was having a hard time understanding what had happened. To her, it was not simply an electoral defeat—it was
as if her father had sustained a personal rebuke. The next
morning, she did not want to go to school. My instinctive
reaction was to say, "Well, this morning I'm going to the
office, and you're going to school, and life goes on."

My parents' overriding consideration when we were young was education. My mother had finished high school and studied nursing, but my father had not completed junior high. For them, education meant a job, a future, in a word, freedom. When we got to the age of fourteen or fifteen, our parents would tell us, "When it comes to your education, we'll pay for everything without a moment's hesitation. For the rest, your clothes, your leisure activities, that is for you to look after." Education was sacred. There was no latitude for taking time off from our studies, for whatever reason. They kept very close tabs on our school work. They didn't expect us to be at the top of our class in every subject. On the contrary, they would say to us, "Look, do your best, but do well, period." I can tell you that on the days when we brought home our report cards, we were on tenterhooks. It was a little like going to confession. My father read our report card and if it was not up to his expectations (which, as I say, were quite reasonable) we were raked over the coals. My father was a very disciplined sort of man. He used to get up early every morning to jog. At that time jogging had not yet come into fashion. For thirty years, he did that every morning of his life, seven days a week. He was exacting, strict, and sometimes quite harsh when things did not go the way he wanted.

About forty years ago my father bought "The Island", on Lake Memphremagog. He built a cottage there a few years later. In the early years there was no electricity and no telephone. Later on we found out that our parents had taken their time installing electricity and a telephone because when you have five young children, no electric light and no television, everybody goes to bed when night falls.

My brother and I were in charge of maintenance in and around the cottage. Every summer we would move to Magog, to what we called The Island. We have wonderful memories of those summers on the lake. My father worked seven days a week but he was close to his family. On

Sundays he often did the cooking. He was an excellent cook—unlike my mother who, if the truth be known, was a terrible cook—largely because of the fact that he once ran a hotel and had had to learn to cook properly, but also because he loved it and was very creative. Every Sunday afternoon my parents would take us for a drive whether we felt like it or not. To my father this was family time, and time spent with the family was sacred. As my grandmother Charest had been widowed quite early, we would go pick her up and take her along for the drive. My father looked after his mother. He made a point of having lunch with her at her home in Rock Forest whenever he could. This family spirit he instilled in us is very much a part of our lives to this day.

Formative Years

I received all of my schooling in French—first from the Soeurs Jésus-Marie and later in the public school system. So my brother and sisters and I grew up in both cultures. Like many young people our own age, we were interested in American music, American television, and we followed American and Canadian politics. At the same time we were becoming aware of francophone culture. I remember one book in particular, *Le Survenant*, by Germaine Guèvremont. It was on the reading list in seventh grade and made a profound impression on me. I savoured every page because its characters reminded me so much of my father's family, my grandfather, some of my uncles and other people I knew. It was then that I understood some of the realities that people like the Charests had experienced and was able to imagine what life for them must have been like. I first became aware of French Québecois culture, as such, through that book. Our teacher was Louise Meunier. Years later, I was to meet her again as the wife of a Tory M.P. named Yvon Côté, elected to Parliament in 1988.

I first met Michèle Dionne, with whom I was to share my life, in junior high. I was fifteen. She was a year older.

We were at École Montcalm together, a school in Sherbrooke whose students had a reputation for being a little unruly. It was the beginning of the seventies—a time of social upheaval in Québec and all over North America, particularly among the young. For me, those were years of growth. I began to take an interest in public life. In Secondary Four (Grade 10), I was elected to represent my classmates on the student council. The following year I lost interest in student politics for a while, but at the end of my final year (Secondary Five, or Grade 11), I was elected president of the student body. A friend, a priest named Bernard Bonneau, suggested I should run. For some reason he thought I would be a good candidate. When the time came, I got cold feet. He literally had to push me onto the stage to deliver my speech. I have been making speeches ever since.

I have to admit I did not study very hard that year. I was more interested in student council affairs. There were 1200 students in the school; we organized student strikes, demonstrations, and conducted negotiations with the teachers. I learned first hand the meaning of public responsibility, which has several dimensions: you learn about conflict resolution, you learn to listen, to hammer out solutions, to scrutinize your own and other people's decisions and, also, when necessary, to say no. You do those things and you accept responsibility for your actions.

During that period I devoted a lot of my time to sporting activities. I skied and, for four years, played soccer. At the time, Sherbrooke had some very good teams that benefited from superb coaching and distinguished themselves at the provincial level. In 1973 we won the Montreal Cup. I was the goalkeeper. Soccer is above all else a team sport. It teaches you to see the world a certain way that is reflected later on in everything you do in life. I was an average student and completed secondary school without distinction. I could have achieved better results if I had applied myself, but at the time I was more interested in student council activities, sports, and rock-and-roll.

With secondary school behind me, I moved on to Collégial (senior high) at the Séminaire de Sherbrooke. I was alone the first year. Michou and I had gone our separate ways. She was at school at Villa Maria in Montreal the first two years, then at Marguerite Bourgeois. She came back to Sherbrooke for her last year of Collégial. I saw her again one night. We have been together ever since. In Collégial, I participated in student politics while preparing to go to university. That said, in my last semester I found I had something like eight credits to make up. In the end I did get my D.E.C (Senior High School Diploma), but I had to pedal hard to get it.

Just before my fourteenth birthday I got my first summer job at a little restaurant in Magog. From the age of fifteen, I worked for several years at the box office of the Centre culturel de l'université de Sherbrooke. It was an unforgettable experience. All the big shows that toured the province in the summertime came to the Centre: Famous theater companies like the Compagnie Jean Duceppe (Jean Duceppe was the father of Bloc Québecois M.P. Gilles Duceppe); ballet companies like the Grands Ballets Canadiens; great comedians like Jean-Guy Moreau; singers like Diane Dufresne; and Québec pop groups like Octobre and Harmonium, not to mention the best foreign films, were all featured attractions. On occasion I was asked to act as stagehand, as the sets, particularly in the case of the Grands Ballets Canadiens, could be quite elaborate. One night, after a performance, I can remember witnessing a memorable row between Jean Duceppe and one of his daughters. They were alone on the stage, yelling at each other as only a father and daughter can. All in all, I tremendously enjoyed the university and cultural scene where I had the opportunity to meet a whole range of people.

When I was twelve I decided I wanted to become a lawyer. At that time, the television series *Perry Mason* was very popular. I used to watch it and say to myself, "That is what I want to do!" Perry Mason, the defender of widows and orphans, was more than a lawyer—he was an advocate with a mission. He was an inspiring role model to me. One night at the dinner table, after watching an episode of *Perry Mason*, I told my parents I had decided what I wanted to do with my life: "I want to be a lawyer." My announcement was greeted with silence. "Why?" my father asked, amused. When I explained myself, he and my mother simply said, "That's what you want to do? Fine. You do that." They were happy with the career I had chosen. My mind was made up. It was what I wanted to do and it did not matter how hard it might be to get there. To me it was not about making money. I wanted the experience of being in a courtroom and pleading before a judge and jury. What mattered to me was to be doing something meaningful—something I believed in.

I began attending the University of Sherbrooke in the fall of 1977. I had been accepted at the University of Ottawa, but I had not been able to get my father to agree to pay for the move. We were at daggers drawn over that. As far as he was concerned, there was no way he was going to cover that kind of expense. At the same time, I was on the University of Sherbrooke waiting list. Three days before the beginning of term, I received word that I had been accepted.

I took my law studies very seriously, mainly because they dealt with a subject that I felt passionate about. I worked hard. It made my father proud. He made a point of driving me to class every morning and picking me up at lunch time. I spent my afternoons studying at home. I lost interest in student politics. I wanted to devote myself exclusively to my studies. Intellectually, I felt stimulated and enriched. The law teaches us to reason, to deal with abstractions, to conduct research, to discriminate, to identify legal precedents, to construct an argument, to plead a case and to persuade a judge and a jury. I was immersed in my studies. My parents were thrilled to see me finally settling down to devote myself to the pursuit of a dream they wholeheartedly approved of.

Then, at Christmas time in 1977, life for me and for my family, my father most of all, changed forever. I was eighteen. My mother suddenly fell gravely ill. She went into hospital at the Centre hospitalier universitaire de Sherbrooke for tests. The doctor, who knew she had been a nurse, gave her the diagnosis: leukemia. He could offer no hope. She had, at most, six months to live. She came home. In her mind, it was all very clear. "I am going to die," she said. "I am going to die within the next six months." We were her children. In our hearts we rebelled against the finality of that verdict. We loved her so much we just could not accept that such a thing should happen to her or that such a calamity should befall us. We spent the months that followed on a roller coaster between unbridled hope when she seemed to get better for a while, and utter despair each time the disease got the better of her. At the first remission we thought she was cured. We lived on hope. We said to ourselves, "Well that's it, then. It's gone."

The summer of 1978 was a miraculous time. It was magnificent—the most beautiful weather of the last twenty years. We were at The Island. The sun shone every day. My mother was able to swim. We spent all our time together. When we found out she was sick again, it was as if the earth had opened up under our feet. My sister Carole, the second-youngest, who was very close to our mother, left school to look after her full time. My father, who had been very brave, sat up with her through the nights. She was in more and more pain. It was heartrending. She was in so much pain that I would end up saying to myself, inside, that this person I worshipped would be better off if she died. I would find myself wishing for her torment to stop, wishing for it to end. Nineteen is an age when you are not very well equipped to deal with emotions such as those. Maybe one never is, but I felt horribly guilty for harbouring such feelings. It got so that one day, sitting in my room, trying to somehow keep my mind on the page I was supposed to be studying, and hearing my mother in the next room, hearing her pain as she called out to me, I suddenly felt paralyzed, unable to move, to stand up, to go to her. That day I lost the courage to face her, to face up to her pain.

It all seemed so unfair. Adolescence is an age when you react very keenly to injustice. We could not accept that this should be happening at a time in her life after she had worked so hard, worried herself so much on our behalf and sacrificed so much to raise us. We took a long time to recover from her death. I do not know whether we ever fully recovered from it. Even today, we find it hard to talk about it amongst ourselves. Her death left a gaping hole in our lives. Later, when I had children, I realized even more how much I miss her. I feel her absence even more because Michou has both her parents. She even has her maternal grandparents. I can see how rich that makes her and how much our lives are enriched by the presence of people who connect us with our past—people who can teach us about who we are.

My father worshipped my mother. He never remarried. Since her death, nothing at home has changed. He still lives there refusing, despite the many invitations we have extended to him, to live anywhere but in the house where she shared his life. When my mother passed away I was studying law. Needless to say my results for the academic year 1977-78 were not the best, but I made up for them the following year. As my mother said, life goes on.

A Sailor's Life

I spent the summer following my mother's death on a laker in the merchant navy. The idea came from a friend who told me that every summer, around the end of June, there was a shortage of labour on board the ships plying the Great Lakes. The job was unionized and well paid. The union was a "closed shop", meaning it, not the employer, did the hiring and that it only hired unionized labour. As Michou had planned to go to Europe on a two-month trip organized by the University of Michigan, I decided to try my luck. So I showed up, three days running, at the local of the International Seamen's Union on St James Street in Montreal. Each time I approached the counter I was ignored. No one would speak to me until one of the two clerks sitting there, a burly, red-haired man, finally cast his baleful stare my way. He just looked at me without a word. I tried to tell him I wanted to join the union, but I felt so nervous I got my words mixed up and mumbled, "I want to get into the syndicate." "WHAT?" roared the man. "I want to get into the syndicate." "Aha", he grunted. Then, turning to his friend, "Hey Charlie! The kid wants to get into the syndicate!" The other fellow shot back, "Tell him to go on Saint-Laurent street and look for white Cadillacs!" Only then did I realize what I had just said. Finally, the next day, he called me over and, at last, I was hired.

It was two in the morning when I stepped on board my first ship, at the Saint-Lambert Lock, as an assistant mechanic. The chief engineer, an Englishman, lost his temper when he saw me. I had no prior experience in the engine room. You have probably seen one of those war movies where men covered in sweat toil at the engines. You are in the hold of a ship twelve stories high. Your watches are four hours long, with eight hours' rest in between. I was fascinated by life on board. A ship constitutes an unique environment. When you are on board a ship, you have no choice but to get along with the people around you. You cannot leave. You cannot avoid them. So there is a special context, I would even say a unique culture, on a ship. When you live it, you feel it. Life on board is very organized, so much so that some sailors, when they leave that life behind, find it difficult to adjust to life ashore. I remember one sailor, a fascinating individual, seventy-six years old, who had tried to retire only to realize that he could not survive anywhere but on a ship. Paying the rent, the phone bill, shopping for groceries and cooking seemed like insurmountable challenges to him. On a boat, those kinds of preoccupations are all taken care of. There is also a rigid hierarchy that is essential for the smooth running of the ship. Everyone has a role. This social organization on board ship is very visible, very tangible. The captain and his officers live on the upper deck. The lower ranks, the sailors, are down in the bottom of the ship.

What really captured my imagination during that first summer was my discovery of Canada and its immense size, splendour and diversity. Our first stop being Québec City, we sailed up the St. Lawrence River. Naturally, I knew no one on board. Because most of the other sailors, who came from all parts of Canada, were not fluent in French, I was called upon right away to act as interpreter and quickly got to know everyone. Next, we stopped at Port

Cartier, which at that time was practically a ghost town. It was the summer of 1979 and I can still remember seeing entire streets lined with boarded up buildings and apartment blocks.[1] I had never seen anything like it. At Port Cartier the ship took on a load of iron ore that we delivered to the port of Cleveland. When I think of Cleveland, I think of a huge port, a big American city, the city Bethlehem Steel. I can remember visiting the downtown core. At seven p.m., the center of Cleveland shuts down— ceases to exist. It empties. The stores close and bars go up on all the shop windows. On every floor of a Cleveland department store, I saw security guards armed with rifles. As for us, it was time to leave.

Working on board ship was a challenge, especially in view of the fact that, being left-handed, I had a knack for always turning the valves in the wrong direction. It was a challenge in other ways as well. I remember an Irish engineer I worked with, who had come over to Canada at the age of five or six, but, whereas I come from a Catholic family, he was a Protestant. One night, when I went below to start my from midnight to four a.m watch, I soon realized he was ignoring me. I was baffled, and then I heard him growl between his teeth, *"You murderer!"* I gaped at him uncomprehendingly. *"That's what you are. A bunch of murderers. YOU KILLED LORD MOUNTBATTEN!"* The I.R.A. had just assassinated Lord Mountbatten, the last Viceroy of India, who had presided over Indian Independence and commanded the British Navy in the Far East during the Second World War, the uncle of Prince Philip and great-uncle of Prince Charles. It took him that entire watch and much of the next day to cool down. In the end, he apologized, saying he had lost his temper and gone too

---

[1] Port-Cartier had been hard hit by the permanent shut-down of the ITT mill in September 1979.

far. It still seems incredible to think of the two of us, so far
away from Ireland, almost coming to blows over an event
that had nothing to do with either of our lives.

It just shows the kind of old resentments you can
carry around like luggage, inherited from previous generations, along with a certain version of history that becomes
part of your culture. That incident reminds me of something my mother used to say to me as a child. If, as
sometimes happened, I came home complaining that
someone that day had called her an "*Anglaise*", my mother
would blanch and protest: "*I am NOT English! Never, never
let anyone say we're English! I am Irish! I am not English!*" We
had no idea where that bitterness was coming from, especially since, in the Townships, French and English got
along well.

The so-called Townshippers were not, for the most
part, wealthy people. They were not the bosses of big
companies. They were mostly shop keepers and factory
workers. Some were well off, others less so. My mother
came from a small English-speaking village in the country.
Her father was a wood merchant. They were not wealthy
people. Even today, in the Eastern Townships, you find
English speakers in all walks of life. They are farmers, small
business people. During elections I meet them at their
factory doors. When those people are your neighbours, it's
a little like on board a ship, you can't afford to ignore
them or allow yourself the luxury of being prejudiced. You
share the same way of life, the same work places, the same
schools. When some tragedy strikes your neighbours, you
cannot afford not to care. You share the same concerns
and the same hopes. That reality became a part of our
lives very early on. Sherbrooke High School was very close
to where we lived. We met its students and its teachers in
the street every day. To put all that into perspective, my
own experience of the relations between anglophones and
francophones is that they were good relations, not entirely

devoid of distrust of course, for our perceptions were a little different. However, there was a social context that created a healthy pressure to get along, to make things work, and to avoid gratuitously criticizing each other. It was like on a ship or in a country. You had to make it work.

But let's get back to the ship. I learned a lot that summer, especially about the Canadian economy. We used to take on a load of iron ore and haul it down to Cleveland, and then sail up to the lakehead at the top of lake Superior. At Thunder Bay, we would take on a load of grain, then sail off again down the Great Lakes and St. Lawrence River all the way to Québec City or Baie-Comeau. That summer, I wrote to my father to tell him I was going to ask for Michou's hand in marriage. I knew he would not like it, that he would say it was not a good idea, that at twenty I was too young. But, as I told him in my letter, my mind was made up and I hoped he would accept, and even support, my decision. As I had a copy of Michou's travel itinerary, I managed to track her down in Greece and, without any warning, asked her, point blank, from a pay phone half way around the world, if she would be my wife. Luckily for me, she said yes. I wrote to her as well. I wrote many letters that summer. I read a lot. I did my reading in between watches. I read a book on the American Bill of Rights. At that time, there was a great deal of debate going on about the possibility of including a Charter of Rights in the Canadian Constitution. Another book I read was *Master Mariner,* by Nicholas Monsarrat, the story of a sailor condemned to go on living through the ages, fighting in all the great wars and witnessing all the great events of human history. More than anything else, I did a lot of thinking. For me, those few months on board the ships were a period of reflection, contemplation, self-discovery and spiritual growth. During this time, I undertook a ten-day fast, which gave me a chance to stop and see my life more clearly.

When I got back to Sherbrooke I returned to my studies. I was in my final year of law. The subjects that most interested me were constitutional law (I got my highest score in that subject), civil liberties (I had an interest, as I said earlier, in the American Bill of Rights), and the writing and interpretation of legislation. I had the good fortune to study under some exceptional professors, including Michael Krauss who now teaches in Washington, D.C. He used to challenge our opinions, compel us to surpass ourselves and teach us to reason for ourselves. Michael Krauss focused our attention on one of the only political issues that really drew my interest as a university student—our system of denominational schools. Michael was a Jewish American. He put the question of religious freedom in education in the context of the University of Sherbrooke, which had its own confessional charter and had chosen to maintain it in order to avoid integration into the Universités du Québec. I became interested in that debate because of my own background. It led me to participate in a committee, at the University of Sherbrooke, which was examining the whole question of the religious denomination of the University.

This concern was reflected when our children were born. We did not have them baptized immediately. It bothered me that, with regard to moral and religious matters, we had let ourselves go on "automatic pilot" in Québec. We are designated Catholic without even knowing why. As the State has taken over a responsibility that should be left up to the individual, we do not have to examine our own moral values or ask ourselves what kind of context we wish to give to them. Personally, I feel this goes a long way toward explaining why the churches are so empty today. In spite of recent constitutional changes allowing for linguistic school boards, which represent obvious progress, the debate on this question is still not settled.

The Halls of Justice

I obtained my Bachelor's degree in law in 1980. The day I received my diploma, I stayed out late celebrating with my friends. Since my father had already gone to bed when I got home, I left my diploma on the corner of the dining room table. The next morning, my father came into my room before I was even awake. He had my diploma in his hands. He was very moved. He said, "You know, your grandfather couldn't read or write." (He had never told me this.) "Your mother would be proud of you."

In the spring of 1980, with diploma in hand, I went back to work on the ships. Michou and I agreed that in order to have enough money to get married, I would have to spend another summer on the Great Lakes. As soon as exams were over, I left for St. Catherine's, Ontario where the International Seamen's Union had an office close to the Welland canal. I boarded a ship that sailed from Windsor to Sault-Sainte-Marie. Meanwhile, in Québec, the referendum campaign on sovereignty-association was in full swing. As I was away, I did not vote in the referendum. However, everyone on board followed the campaign. There were vigorous debates. Sometimes tempers flared. People's sensibilities were a little raw and you had to be careful. On board ship is where I first met people from all over Canada. I especially remember my first contact with a chef from Newfoundland. I could not understand a word he was saying! I said to myself "Where does he come from?" There were some real characters from Cape Breton as well. I had to learn to understand them too. It was quite an education.

In short, the referendum took place, I came back ashore for three days, just long enough to get married, spent forty-eight hours in Québec City (a two-day honeymoon!), and then returned to my ship.

The last ship I sailed on belonged to Canada Steamship Lines, a company owned by Paul Martin. I worked twelve hours a day, seven days a week, and had become a more seasoned sailor than the year before. So, when we went through the lock at Beauharnois, I disembarked knowing I had exactly twenty-four hours to catch up with my ship at Québec City. Michou would be waiting in our Austin Mini her parents had given her. We would drive down to Sherbrooke, spend a few hours together, and speed on up to Québec City to wait for the pilot boat to take me back to the ship. By the end of the summer I had saved up quite a bit of money. Michou and I could also count on some student bursaries and loans. So I set about preparing for admission to the Bar while continuing to work at a branch of the Société des Alcools. I have to say our budget that year was pretty tight. By spring, our cupboards were nearly bare and our money had almost run out. We started doing the rounds of our families. My parents-in-law found that we came around more often for supper. And my father would say, "Isn't that nice of you to come more often to visit me." The truth was we were beginning to run out of money.

That year Michou began to work as a Special Education teacher. I began practicing law, at first with legal aid in the criminal law section. That kind of practice has a high volume caseload. You are in court every day. You plead in

Municipal Court, before Justices of the Peace, in Superior
Court and at the Court of Appeal. Later, I joined the firm
of Michel Beauchemin and Michel Dussault in Sherbrooke. I practiced criminal law in the same high volume
way, but in an atmosphere that was extremely competitive.
It was the period immediately following the introduction
of the Canadian Charter of Rights and Freedoms. While
studying law, I had been very interested in the American
Bill of Rights. As I was a beginner, and was often up against
more experienced colleagues, I made sure I was prepared,
even if it meant staying up all night. When I appeared in
Court the next day, I had stacks of legal precedents in my
arsenal. It was a learning experience. Lawyers who practice
criminal law will tell you they are faced with a degree of
human misery one does not normally see. I realized later
that I had been very young to come into contact with the
world of crime. At twenty-one or twenty-two, when you
have been raised in a loving, stable home with plenty of
discipline and strong moral values, you are ill-prepared to
confront harsh social realities. Claude Leblond, my first
employer at legal aid, thought I was spending too much
time interviewing my clients in my office trying to help
them. He wisely said to me, "Jean, your client is entitled to
the best possible service from his lawyer. If you try to
become his social worker, you are depriving him of the
services of a good lawyer. Look after the legal side of
things and leave the social work to his case worker." It was
sound advice.

The court room taught me about human nature and
the human condition. There I discovered the very serious
problem of illiteracy, which I had never suspected could
be so widespread in a modern, industrialized country like
Canada. My clients were often young men between the
ages of fifteen and twenty-five who did not know how to
read or write, and, because of that, lived in a kind of social
prison. In many cases they suffered from extreme poverty

and a lack of social maturity that made them incapable of dealing with the petty conflicts and frustrations one encounters in every day life. But you could not just sit in judgment. You had to try and understand them. It grieved me to see so many young people my own age in such dire straights. One of the first cases I pleaded concerned a young man who had a drug and alcohol problem. At that time there were no resources in Québec to help young men like him. There was nowhere you could send him. For example, Portage, which at that time took in adults, had not begun specializing in the treatment of adolescents who cannot be treated in the same way as adults.

These early experiences made a lasting impression on me and certainly influenced my political life. Later, as Minister of State for Youth, I was to take a very keen interest in the development of literacy programs, such as Stay in School, designed to address the problems of dropouts. Throughout my career, the difficulties young people face have remained one of my paramount concerns.

The Will to Serve

I had pleaded about eight cases before a judge and jury when I was offered a position in a large law firm in Sherbrooke specializing in labour law. I declined the offer sensing I was not going to be able to enjoy the kind of freedom I wanted. Maybe, in that way I was a little like my father who always felt the need to be his own boss, to be self-sufficient and the master of his own affairs. Around the same time I was once again beginning to take an interest in public life. I was twenty-four. I had reached a crossroads. I remembered what my mother told me about the need to give my life meaning. By this time I knew that I did not want to spend the rest of my days as a criminal lawyer. It was not an environment in which I thought I could accomplish the things I wanted to do. On the other hand, maritime law appealed to me. I made inquiries about applying to take a Master's degree in Maritime Law at Tulane University in Louisiana. My experience on board ship had made such an impression on me that I thought this field of law would be an interesting area in which to work. For her part, Michou was interested in a program for teaching French in Louisiana, which was set up by the Québec Ministry of Education.

Meanwhile, every Sunday night we went to my father's for supper, either at the house or the cottage. My brother Robert, our father and myself would often take a few minutes in the kitchen to talk about all sorts of things, politics included. One Sunday, my father reminded us that the Tory party convention had just been held in Winnipeg. There had been a vote of confidence that the leader, Joe Clark, had judged inconclusive. He then convened a leadership convention. Knowing that I was interested in politics, my father turned to me and said, "Well, now is the time to get involved. Things are going to get interesting." I made a few calls to find out who in Sherbrooke was a Tory supporter. Pierre Gagné, a Sherbrooke forensic psychiatrist who was active in the Conservative Party, recommended that I speak to Denis Beaudoin, the organizer for Joe Clark in the area. I was actually more interested in Brian Mulroney's candidacy, but those decisions are sometimes made in an unusual way. People tend to underestimate the importance of the human factor in politics. Political scientists in particular sometimes give too much emphasis to the theoretical aspect. In a race for delegates to a leadership convention, it is often first come, first served. Beaudoin came to see me and reminded me of the passion with which Joe Clark had staunchly defended Québec's position at the time of the patriation of the Constitution, and I found his argument convincing. I had closely followed events surrounding the adoption of the 1982 Constitution. To the francophone Québecer in me, Québec's place in Canada was of paramount interest, and I liked the opinions Joe Clark had expressed on the subject. All those elements taken together helped me to decide to support his leadership.

At the time, Michou was pregnant with Amélie, our first child. When I came home after my meeting with Denis Beaudoin and told her I had decided to get involved in the delegate-selection process leading up to the leadership convention, she was worried. She didn't like politics. She came from a rather Liberal family and took a very dim view of the whole thing. Knowing me as she did, she knew I was going to give it all I had. Beaudoin had some good advice for me. He told me the only way to resolve everything was for Michou to get involved as well. This, of course, was not easy, as she was pregnant. The delegate selection meeting, which our side won, took place a day or two after the birth of our daughter Amélie. We had sold a lot of membership cards. In spite of the fact that Mulroney's campaign in the region was run by Pierre-Claude Nolin, we managed to win the slate. So I went and celebrated in the hospital with Michou. I even pasted Joe Clark stickers on the door of her hospital room.

The convention was to be held in June, so it allowed us to take our first holiday together after the birth of Amélie. Michou had come along saying she would lend a hand, but in the end she became really involved. For the duration of the convention she arose at four in the morning to slip Joe Clark leaflets under hotel room doors. Ironically, she was part of the team that, along with my sister-in-law Louise Lareau, decorated the ball room for Joe Clark's victory party, which never took place. Ten years later, almost to the day, in the same ballroom, we were the ones conceding defeat to the leader chosen by Conservative party members to lead them into battle in 1993. Joe Clark supported me, just as I had supported him ten years earlier.

For Michou, on a personal level, that June convention in 1983 was a revelation. She had fun, and from that day forward has shared fully and enthusiastically in my commitment to public life. Fortunately for me, we did it all together. Otherwise, life in politics would be very tough. As for me, I had just entered a new arena where I felt it would be possible, with conviction, hard work and perseverance, to effect change, make a difference, and influence the course of events. I realized that I cared about making this country work. I believed, and still believe, very strongly in the partnership that is Canada.

I was recently criticized for saying that it was thanks to that partnership that French-speaking Québecers have managed to retain their language, their culture and their own way of doing things. Instead of becoming assimilated into the American melting-pot, our population has increased from 60,000 in 1763, at the time the Treaty of Paris was signed, to six and a half million—seven and a half million including francophones in other parts of Canada—one quarter of the total population. Why? Let's look at our history. In 1774, almost a hundred years before Confederation, the Québec Act guaranteed francophones the right to their language, their religion and their civil law. You have to put yourself in the context of the time. A pre-revolutionary situation existed in the Thirteen Colonies to the south. It was two years before the American Declaration of Independence. In that context, England realized she had no hope of retaining her North American possessions unless she concluded an agreement with the francophones who lived in this part of the continent. For their part, our ancestors had the intelligence and foresight to understand that they had a choice between ensuring their cultural survival or taking the risk of being absorbed into a new, English-speaking Republic. It was this pact, rooted in a lucid recognition of mutual interests, that formed the basis of the Canadian partnership.

Despite the ups and downs of our history, this pact has held. But who ever said that, because we maintained our right and freedom to speak our language, to teach it to our children, to use it before our courts of law and in our legislative assembly, that it was going to be easy or that we would not have to be ever vigilant, given the North American context, in order to ensure that our language and our culture continued to be handed down to future generations? Yes, we have had to wage an unrelenting struggle to ensure the survival of our language and our culture. Without the partners and the leaders we selected for ourselves throughout our history, we would have suffered the same fate as francophones in New England and Louisiana.

The often made mistake is to fixate on past conflicts, mistakes and disagreements as if they were the rule rather than the exception. The Act of Union was probably not the idea of the century as far as francophones are concerned. But then it did not work—it was not a success. It was the kind of mistake that some of us should stop showcasing as though they have become the reality in this country. The real story is that the fledgling Canada became a democracy with a responsible government. Political parties quickly realized that in order to govern, i.e. to get a majority in the legislative assembly, French and English had to respect each other and work together.

The other dimension that is often overlooked is that in a relationship you have to work at making it right. It isn't by folding our arms, criticizing one another, and hurling accusations and blame, that we can resolve disagreements and keep moving forward. In politics, as in relationships, nothing is ever finished. Some Canadians, including some Québecers, get a little impatient with the question of national unity and ask, "Will it never end?" But ask yourself this: would you ever think of sitting down with your spouse one fine morning and saying, "Today, dear, we are going to have a discussion, and afterward, it will be over; all our problems will be solved; we will never have to talk any more. We are both twenty-eight years old, but from now on we are never going to have another discussion as long as we live?" That is not how things work in a relationship, be it a marriage, a business, or a country.

The Apprenticeship
of Power

When the Progressive Conservative association for the riding of Sherbrooke convened on May 15, 1984 to pick a candidate for the federal election, I was not the favourite. My opponent, Claude Métras, who at fifty was twice my age and would have made a very good M.P, had the backing of the Party. I had to fight, and the experience taught me many things. In a race for the Party nomination, you are on your own. It is a test. You have to prove yourself by demonstrating your resourcefulness, organizational skills and ability to attract supporters and mount a successful campaign. In politics you have to rely on yourself, to set your own agenda and identify priorities to a much greater extent than most people realize. The nomination meeting in Sherbrooke was hotly contested. It was a sign of what the election held in store. No matter what the polls say, it is a sure sign of the strength of a party when the field is crowded in a nomination race.

At the time I was chosen as the Conservative candidate in the riding of Sherbrooke, John Turner had just become leader of the federal Liberal Party, which immediately shot up in public opinion polls. The election soon followed. When the vote was called the Conservatives were far behind in Québec. Nevertheless, certain trends, such

as the desire for change, run deep, even when they are
momentarily masked by opinion polls. In 1984, the
Liberals had been in power for a very long time, and in
the eyes of the electorate their mandate had expired. You
could also sense a desire for reconciliation, a need to
turn the page, after a divisive debate on the future of the
country. All these factors combined to produce a campaign such as one rarely sees in one's lifetime. There was a
wave, which is fantastic for those riding the crest of the
wave, but disastrous for those being swept before it. You
learn a great deal in such times. When you arrive in the
House of Commons, for the first few months you are
bursting with pride. You look down on your opponents.
You are a little blinded by it all. With the passage of time
you realize that the true merit of sitting in the House lies
less with those who rode the wave than with those who
managed to survive it. However, it takes years to learn and
appreciate that simple fact. Some never do learn and
suffer the consequences.

I was fortunate at the beginning of my political career.
I was twenty six and new to Parliament, but Prime Minister
Mulroney had received favourable reports of my performance from people close to him, such as Michael
Meighen, who later became a Senator, and George Maclaren, who was one of my close friends in Sherbrooke. He
named me Assistant Deputy Speaker of the House of
Commons, a lengthy title that meant I was one of four
M.P.'s (the Speaker, his Deputy, and two Assistant Deputies)
who arbitrate debates in the House. This was a wonderful
opportunity for a beginner like me. I had a reserved seat
from which to closely observe the intricate workings of the
Canadian Parliament. It allowed me to appreciate the
quality of that forum and to get to know its best orators—
and its worst. I learned the importance of knowing the
rules of the House. A member of Parliament, no matter
how competent, cannot afford to lose face in the House.

That being said, you do not necessarily have to distinguish yourself at Question Period to be effective in politics. Not everyone can be a great parliamentarian in the classic sense, but you cannot allow yourself to fail in that arena. If you do, all your other achievements may be suddenly eclipsed.

On a more personal note, Michou and I made some decisions that turned out to be wise. Denis Beaudoin, who had managed my campaign, gave us some excellent advice. He was the son of an M.P. (his father, Léonel Beaudoin, had been the Crédit Social M.P. for the riding of Richmond). Both he and his father strongly recommended that we move to Ottawa. Our daughter Amélie was a year and a half at the time. They told us that if we wanted to give our marriage every chance of success, and to ensure that my political career made room for a rewarding family life, we should go live in Ottawa and say so publicly. Tell the people of Sherbrooke why you are doing this, they said. After that, it will be up to you to prove that you are serving them well. But avoid creating a situation where people find out a year after the fact that they have been gradually abandoned. We took that advice, and it was one of the best decisions we could have made. First, because it made us closer, and second, because it allowed us to spend a maximum of time together and with our children. However, that transition demanded a lot of Michou. When she arrived in Ottawa she did not speak English as well as she would have liked. She also had to make sacrifices with regard to employment.

I spent my first two years in Ottawa familiarizing myself with Parliamentary work. Again, I received excellent advice. For example, there are several parliamentary associations in Ottawa. Friends recommended that I join the Canada-U.S. Inter-Parliamentary Association. There are other parliamentary associations of great value, but this was the most important in terms of the issues and the people you met. On the eve of a debate on Free Trade, this forum allowed me to familiarize myself with issues that concerned both countries and to get to know some of the actors involved. All of this was very useful to me when I became Minister of the Environment.

This first part of my 1984 to 1988 mandate was significant because of a local problem in my riding, which I was called upon to help resolve. The Domtar plant in Windsor (Québec) had been refused a federal grant for modernizing its installations, which had raised a storm of protest in the region. As I was a member of the government and an M.P. from the Eastern Townships, my skills as the people's representative were put to the test. I learned then to differentiate between what is essential and what is secondary. My first priority had to be to defend the interests of my region and of the people who had elected me and to do it with vigour, from inside the government, without becoming a dissident within its ranks.

Those first two years also taught me to appreciate the value of experience. The Québec Conservative caucus had very few experienced M.P.s. At first, when a political storm broke out, it was hard for us to tell the difference between a passing cloudburst and a potential hurricane. It was difficult to know whether or not an event that was making the headlines on a given day was going to have long term consequences, and we paid a price for that. The Mulroney government as a whole paid a price for its inexperience during the first four years of its mandate. Those are lessons you never forget. Early on, I learned to seek the advice of experienced people who could guide me by helping me recognize issues that could have implications for the long term and understanding the consequences of my political actions.

The Youth Issue

Then came the Cabinet shuffle of June 25, 1985. It was a major overhaul that aimed to give the government a new momentum, a new image and a new energy. The day after my twenty-eighth birthday I became Minister of State for Youth. The government was almost half-way through its mandate. I arrived in a ministry that had been in the spotlight because of cuts the government had made, particularly to a program called Katimavik. Liberal Senator Jacques Hébert even went on a hunger strike to protest the cuts.

Prime Minister Mulroney had decided to alter the structure of his ministry by transferring the Ministry of State for Youth from the Ministry of State to that of Employment and Immigration, a huge department then numbering some 22,000 civil servants. In so doing, he was signaling that his government was making the problem of youth unemployment a priority. He asked me to prepare a comprehensive Youth Policy. He had already set up a working group, chaired by Québec business executive Michel Gaucher and made up of experts from outside the government, to make recommendations concerning a Youth Policy to the federal government.

The Youth portfolio taught me a great deal about the structure of government. The trend at the time was to create ministries of State in an effort to reflect the concerns of society at large. For example, if the problems of young people became a major political issue, you created a Ministry of State. In the same way you will not be surprised to learn that a Ministry of State for Senior Citizens was later created. But the price you paid for destructuring the government in this way, to give different groups in society more access, was a structure that was less cohesive. What you gained by being more accessible, you lost in efficiency and political will within the government apparatus. In practical terms, I was being asked to coordinate everything the government did with regard to youth. However, I soon realized that it is well near impossible to coordinate from the bottom up. Coordination only works from the top down because the top is where the authority lies, and by that I particularly mean moral authority. Some time later, when the newly elected Bourassa government in Québec City was considering the creation of a Ministry of Youth in Québec, we were asked what our experience had been. We recommended, if they really wanted to make a difference, that they create a secretariat within the Conseil Exécutif (the Premier's own department). That way the coordination of the various programs, in the different departments that were meant to help young people, would benefit from the full moral clout of the Premier himself. That, we told them, would really work.

Meanwhile, we were left to ourselves. Ministers of State receive their mandate from their Senior Minister. In my case, the Minister of Employment and Immigration was Benoît Bouchard. In human terms, it was a little like forcing two children to share the same sandbox and telling one of them, "You're in charge." I am oversimplifying, but the fact remains that the relationship between a Senior Minister and his or her Minister of State is often difficult. Negotiating my mandate with Benoît Bouchard took some time. At the outset, I was responsible for the summer employment program for students, but I finally obtained what I wanted, i.e. the responsibility of preparing the Youth Policy the Prime Minister had requested. I had the good fortune of working with John Edwards, a deputy minister of exceptional talent. It was at that time I learned to fully appreciate the Canadian Public Service. We are fortunate in Canada to have an extremely competent body of civil servants who are capable of contributing substantially to our country's development. I mention it because, in terms of our international competitiveness, we often underestimate the importance of having a public service worthy of our aspirations. The size of government and bureaucratic inefficiency are separate issues. What I am talking about is the advantage of having, within the government, men and women who are competent and capable of assisting those who govern in preparing their decisions.

Which brings me to add that you cannot blame the civil servants for a poor administration. What I have learned from experience is that civil servants like nothing better than to have a strong minister. It is in the interest of each department to have a minister who is capable of promoting his initiatives at the Cabinet table. The reverse is also true. If a minister is weak, has no plan and has no idea of what he or she wants to do, as nature abhors a vacuum, civil servants are bound to fill it. You cannot expect them not to. Naturally they will push policies and priorities they consider to be right according to their own perspectives—policies that are not necessarily those of a government elected by the people to represent the whole of the electorate. You cannot blame them. To me, the conclusion is obvious. It is up to the politicians to shoulder their responsibilities while ensuring they attract the most competent people to the public service.

The civil servants in my department were a revelation. They worked incredibly hard to help me construct the Youth Policy the Prime Minister had requested. In terms

of the methodology involved, I learned that there are a
series of steps you have to go through in order to design
the kinds of policies that are likely to meet the tests of
reality in any lasting way. The real test of the value of a
policy is whether it is pertinent enough to outlast its
initiators. When a government puts a policy in place and it
outlives that government, that is a true indication of
its worth.

The first thing we did was define the issues. There
had been a hue and cry around the Katimavik cuts.
However, I discovered that in the past very little had been
done to try and identify the underlying issues that were of
concern to the younger generation of Canadians. In
Canada, and everywhere else, the issues change with each
generation. I never bought the idea that there was a "lost
generation". The reality is that every generation has different problems. You have to be lucid enough to recognize
them and then give yourself the means to address them. In
the case at hand, the most important issues facing young
people were education, training, and the transition from
school to the workforce.

To fully appreciate the challenge with which we were
faced, it is important to realize that, in Canada, we had
until very recently been living in a relatively simple economy based almost entirely on our natural resources. I
recalled my experience aboard the ships: on the Great
Lakes we took on iron ore at Port Cartier or Sept-Îles
bound for Chicago or Cleveland, where it was transformed
into steel to make cars and other manufactured goods; or
we picked up a load of grain at Thunder Bay and delivered
it to Baie-Comeau to be loaded onto ships bound for
overseas. You could say what I experienced first hand was
what the Canadian economy was all about. Now I was
discovering that unlike other industrialized countries that
were our competitors, we had not made much of an effort
to give ourselves transition mechanisms between school

and the workforce, such as mentorship, workplace training and cooperative teaching programs that made it possible to combine work and study.

At the time, we ordered an in-depth survey of public opinion in Canada regarding the expectations of young people and their parents that uncovered a considerable gap between expectations and reality. For example, 80% of parents expected their children to attend university, whereas only 13 or 14% of their children actually pursued their education beyond secondary school. This gap between reality and expectations presaged major disappointments for many young people and their families. People needed to be better informed. At the same time, ways had to be found to better understand the problems we faced in relation to the solutions that were at hand. We got to work and the first thing we did was to draw up, in a general way, a canvas of the needs of young people. At this early stage, we did not necessarily determine whether questions fell under federal or provincial jurisdiction.

The next thing we did was ask ourselves what were the best ways, within the Federal government's areas of responsibility, to provide solutions in response to the needs we had identified. I soon reached the conclusion: in a federation such as ours, one of the roles that the Federal government can legitimately play is to set objectives for the country as a whole—and that will necessarily transcend jurisdictions. The Prime Minister may legitimately identify issues, which are important to all Canadians, and encourage the whole country to undertake initiatives for the purpose of overcoming obstacles that hinder Canada's competitiveness in relation to other countries of the world.

From this perspective, even though education is an exclusive provincial jurisdiction, there is no reason why the Prime Minister of Canada cannot say, "education is important to us as a country." He even has a moral responsibility to say it. It is the prerogative of the head of government to set the agenda and to define the issues of his or her times. Having done so, his or her duty is to persuade the electorate. After that, the challenges become practical ones, and the Federal government has to respect every one's role. While it is perfectly legitimate for the Canadian government to say that education is important, this does not mean that it should try to take the place of provincial governments in their areas of jurisdiction. That would be a terrible mistake. To try and do for someone else what they should be doing for themselves may seem to respond to a political imperative in the short term, but, in the long term, it actually creates more problems than it resolves. Roles become blurred and needed solutions, which should be coming from those who are responsible for providing them, are delayed.

The obvious conclusion was to examine the means available to the Federal government to reach young people in need. In that respect, its biggest lever, the one that has the most impact, was the unemployment insurance system (now known as employment insurance). A considerable share of the money earmarked for people between the ages of 18 and 34 came from this fund. In fact, the socio-economic profile of the people drawing unemployment insurance revealed that the vast majority of them had not completed Grade Ten. The rule that applied then, and still applies now, was simple: the higher the level of education or training a person had achieved, the more likely he or she would be to be holding a well-paying job.

Consequently, the Youth Policy I proposed to the Federal government aimed first to encourage young people to stay in school. It is also why the primary tool that I was trying to develop in order to achieve this objective was the Unemployment Insurance fund. This required the federal government to put itself at the service of an objective that was going to be decided by each provincial government. This had to be recognized and accepted.

Furthermore, the Youth Policy I was proposing was pretty radical for a government in 1988 since it advocated nothing less than a complete overhaul of unemployment insurance rules with regard to young people. To implement it, the federal government would have had to change its unemployment insurance legislation, which would no longer have applied in the same way to young people as it did to everyone else.

The other consequence of such a policy was that the government would have to spend more money. We planned, for example, to expand funding for guidance programs. Not enough was being done to help young people plan for the future or to inform them of the available choices. We wanted to spend more money to help them go back to school, to integrate them into training programs, to enable them to gain experience in the workplace, and to develop a range of options that were compatible with their needs, which could vary widely. The problem of unemployment among the young is much more complex than the old saying "no experience, no job; no job, no experience" would have us believe. For some, a lack of experience on entering the workforce can be an asset. Some employers actually prefer to hire people they can train on the job, people who do not yet have ingrained work habits that they first have to discard before they can learn new ones.

The primary aims of the Youth Policy I wanted the government to adopt were the following: each young person in Canada would either be in school, in a training program, employed or doing community work. Our objective would be that no young persons would be left to themselves without being offered some meaningful form of help. It also meant that a young person who chose not to participate actively in this collective effort would not receive the same level of support. That way there was a very clear incentive aimed at encouraging self-reliance and responsibility. The other dimension of this policy was practical: the federal government was going to have to administer a major federal program in accordance with objectives that would be set, jointly, where possible, if not entirely, by its provincial partners.

"This is Frank McKenna"

So, the debate began within the Cabinet. What I
didn't know was that, within the government, my Youth
Policy was not taking off. I believed in it, and the department believed in it, but in the Finance department it was
seen as too unwieldy, too complicated, and too expensive.
It was not in the general tone of the government. In other
departments it sparked little or no interest. That is the
crux of the problem for anyone attempting to coordinate
policy from the bottom up. It did not matter that we had
crafted a major policy initiative. It did not matter that we
had done all our homework. It was going nowhere.
Looking back, what is interesting to me about that experience is that although I was told "No" several times at
various stages in the process, I refused to listen because I
was so convinced that what I was proposing made sense. I
learned an important lesson at my expense, which is that
in government you are never told "No" directly. There are
all kinds of subtler ways of letting you know that your
project is in limbo. The hinting is discreet and round-
about. Stubborn as I was, I was unwilling to decipher the
true meaning of the messages I was receiving.

I persevered, which generated a certain uneasiness
within the government because no matter how many

procedural steps I cleared only to be sent back to the drawing board, I just kept charging back. In the end, Prime Minister Mulroney had to intervene and try to arbitrate. Obviously, he had been told "Charest's proposal is not moving ahead and it's getting to be a pain." The Prime Minister, not wishing to curb my enthusiasm, congratulated me on the work I was doing and announced, at a Cabinet meeting, in front of all my colleagues, that he was naming someone from the Privy Council Office to help me pilot the project. Delighted by that assurance, I went back to the department thinking that was it, that the whole thing was in the bag, only to realize, when I mentioned the name of the person the Prime Minister had chosen, that person's goal was not going to be to see my proposal through, but to bury it.

We went on like this, never advancing very far until, as often happens in politics, sudden, sheer luck intervened. A First Ministers' Conference was scheduled to be held in Toronto in November, 1987. A few days before that date, a meeting of federal and provincial ministers responsible for the labour market was due to take place in Newfoundland. As there was little enthusiasm for my proposal within the federal government, and since no one had actually brought themselves to tell me so directly, it was suggested that I take it up with the provincial ministers. If I could persuade them to come onboard, so much the better, as my initiative required close cooperation between the two levels of government. "We'll catch the ball on the fly and carry it from there," I was told. It was even hinted that if I managed to convince my provincial colleagues, my proposal could be brought up at the First Ministers' Conference, which is the political *ne plus ultra* for anyone hoping to get something done. The ultimate dynamic within government is really a contest to see who will succeed in getting their proposal on the Prime Minister's desk. It all comes down to a frantic race, a fierce struggle within the government apparatus that turns it into a real jungle. The work desk of a head of government is a limited space. The head of government cannot undertake twenty different initiatives at the same time and hope to achieve success. He or she generally selects three or four, which become priorities for the government. So anyone who manages to get their issue included on the agenda wins the day. All the others can only circle the table hoping to get the nod sooner or later. What I was looking for was a way to get my proposal on Mulroney's desk.

The scenario was that if I succeeded in getting a consensus at the meeting of federal and provincial ministers, the file would be referred to the First Ministers' Conference. We would have won our bet, and the government would be obliged to follow up on our proposal. The ministers' meeting in Newfoundland was a disappointment. I realized that recent spending cuts by the Federal government to the provinces had created an environment that made it practically impossible for me to convince my provincial colleagues to support this new initiative. Some objected on jurisdictional grounds, others just did not believe in it, still others did not see it as a priority for their government, period. Of course what I was suggesting was not a bad concept, except that they had other ideas and were going to do other things. As they could not do twenty things at once, they said, "It's too bad, but the timing is wrong."

So it did not work. Except that a new government had just been elected in New Brunswick (at the meeting in Newfoundland, the minister, who had been sworn in a few days before, had reacted very negatively to my proposal). A few days after the meeting, I got a phone call at my riding office from a Mr. McKenna. As there was a florist by that name in Sherbrooke with whom I often did business, I took the call thinking I was speaking to the florist's son. "John, how are you?" I said. There was a pause. "This isn't

John. This is Frank." I had a moment's hesitation. Frank? Frank? I tried to think. Who in the McKenna family was named Frank? Finally I heard, "This is the Premier of New Brunswick." Oops, sorry.

When you are a junior minister, you rarely get a phone call from the Premier of a province. I was flattered, but I was even more delighted when McKenna told me he had taken a look at my proposal and found it very interesting. He understood what others had not, which was that the proposal was a completely new policy initiative involving new money. Coming right to the point, he told me my proposal was completely in line with what he was planning to do in New Brunswick; his government wanted to participate; he wanted to work closely with me; and he asked me how he could help move things along. I answered that there was a First Ministers' Conference coming up, and that it would be a very timely opportunity to bring the proposal forward. "Right away," he told me. "That's exactly what I am going to do. Send me all the relevant documents. I'll see it's put on the agenda." I could not believe my good fortune.

Where we had thought we were no longer in the running, we now suddenly found our project not only on the table, but sponsored by an unexpected ally. This situation also often happens in politics: you find yourself getting help from unforeseen allies or facing adversaries you thought were your friends. Over at the Prime Minister's Office when I told them the good news, I quickly realized that in their eyes it was anything but. The reality was that in preparation for these top-level meetings between heads of governments, topics for discussion, as well as ultimate objectives and outcomes, are always defined well in advance. Now, all of a sudden, the thing resurfaces, a matter everyone thought settled, but no, it's back... I soon understood they were not happy and even suspected collusion between us and the government of New

Brunswick. We had a job convincing them that we were sincere, and that there had not been any kind of manipulation on our part. Luckily, Mulroney, as was his wont, took me aside and said, "Come on, we're going to move this thing forward." I contacted some of the other premiers like Grant Devine of Saskatchewan and Bill Van der Zalm of British Columbia. My discussions with them made it possible to follow up on my proposal, but I cannot say that they gave it strong backing.

In order for a policy initiative to reach the implementation stage, the government has to believe in it. Support for it within the government has to be both widespread and firm, that is to say quantitative in terms of the number of ministers who support it, and quantitative in that their support is strong enough for them to be willing to defend it. The proposal has to be able to hold the road regardless of whatever obstacles will inevitably arise. In the end, once we got the attention of the First Ministers, we found ourselves back at square one. The First Ministers discussed it because McKenna had pushed it onto the agenda, but in many cases it was given little more than courteous lip-service—speeches for the sake of appearances. For who indeed at a First Ministers' Conference was going to come out and say they were turning down a proposal to help young people? The end result was a compromise, but that merits a chapter in itself.

"Control him!"

We were entering the fourth year of our mandate. Elections would soon have to be called. Now it was urgent to get my proposal off the ground. In the months that followed, the battle at the Cabinet level went into the last round and ended on a humorous note. At this final stage, discussions are arbitrated by a senior minister (in this case Jake Epp) who chairs a Cabinet committee. The main actors in this negotiation are the person making the proposal, those with objections, those wanting changes, and each player trying to mould the proposal to his or her own views to draw the maximum benefit from it for his or her department. It should be said that Cabinet committees were one of the essential components of the Mulroney government. In this regard, it was almost as important to know who chaired each committee of the Cabinet as it was to know who was minister of each department. One example of this is the Treasury Board: If you are a member of the Treasury Board, you have clout because it is the nerve center of the government; no ministerial decision is implemented without the agreement of the Treasury Board. If you are a minister who sits on the Treasury Board, your colleagues had better solicit your support.

My policy proposal had thus reached the penultimate stage before going to Cabinet for approval. The meeting began with a bang. Instead of delegating his junior minister to represent him, as one would have expected given the relative importance of the matter under discussion, the Finance Minister himself showed up at the meeting. My assistant gave me a nudge, and when I saw his expression I suddenly realized we were in for a rough ride. Michael Wilson had come in person to express his reservations. The very fact that he was there sent an unequivocal message: We had just hit a wall. Two days later, as I was pressing on regardless, still stubbornly refusing to hear the whole range of euphemisms for "No" that had now been conveyed to me, there was yet one last step to clear. It involved putting the finishing touches on the final document, called a Record of Decision, that was going to be submitted to Cabinet for final approval. At this final stage, the committee chair presents a draft of the Record of Decision, which is prepared in advance by officials in the Privy Council Office (the department of the Prime Minister). What follows is a meticulous discussion over precise wording. A few hours before this crucial meeting was to take place, the Privy Council Office sent over a copy of the draft Record of Decision that was going to be discussed. When I read it with my two assistants, it became obvious that my Youth Policy, for which I had been battling for many months, had just been killed. We felt dejected and dispirited. We had lost.

Facing failure, I suddenly asked myself why the discussion had to be held on the basis of the document I had been sent. Why indeed not draft a Record of Decision of our own? My assistants and I spent the lunch hour preparing a document that, in its form, was a complete facsimile of the one we had received. But its substance was changed. I mapped out a strategy: let the meeting begin, start the discussion on the wording, wait until everyone gets a little bogged down in details, and then, at an opportune moment, i.e. when there was enough confusion around the table, pull out my own draft as a way out of the deadlock. At the time, my associate deputy-minister, John Edwards, had been replaced. I was to be accompanied to the meeting by Nick Mulder, an intelligent, energetic man who obviously wanted to assist me to the best of his ability, but whom I did not yet know very well.

The meeting began, and the first half-hour unfolded as I had expected. We reviewed the text sentence by sentence, changing a word here, a paragraph there. We got hung up on commas and semi-colons. Lines were crossed out. Our copies filled up with arrows and addenda in the margins. Then, when everyone seemed sufficiently exasperated, I offered some unexpected relief. "If you'll allow me," I said, "I have another version to submit." As I had hoped, Jake Epp, whom I knew well, leapt at the opportunity. Just then, Nick Mulder, whom I had forgotten to inform of my intentions, leaned over and whispered, "What is this?"

"It's our own version," I whispered back.

"What version? What do you mean?"

"The version we drafted."

"You didn't do that!"

"Yes, we did."

"*But you can't do that!*"

"Why not?"

"*Because you are the Minister!*"

It was like an episode of the famous British satirical television series *Yes, Minister!* about a rather simple-minded minister and his machiavellian deputy. After the meeting, Mulder was furious. "How could you do that!" he fumed. "You are the Minister!—Yes, but *it's not up to you to do that!* You can't draft your own decisions!" The Privy Council Office lost no time in contacting Mulder. They were beside themselves. "Your Minister is out of control!" they said. "Control him!" As for me and my assistants, we couldn't stop laughing.

In conclusion, as the elections were getting closer, the Cabinet finally agreed to two pilot projects: one in New Brunswick and the other in Newfoundland, for which the Federal government earmarked 70 million and 54 million dollars respectively. The McKenna government made theirs into an important program. Together we opened ten Youth centers in New Brunswick, offering guidance counseling to young people on Unemployment Insurance or Welfare in order to direct them to the resources that could best assist them in finding their place in the workforce.

What is important to me is that governments and society at large recognize the value of work not merely in economic terms. There is not enough recognition, in Canada as well as in other parts of the industrialized world, of the social, moral and spiritual value of work. We only fully take part in society when we work in the broadest sense of the word. Someone who chooses to stay at home to raise a family contributes in an essential way to the common good. The same goes for someone who does unpaid community work. The workplace itself is constantly changing. The values relating to it are also evolving. It is no longer true to say that we work just to earn a living or purchase consumer goods. Society has changed since the beginning of the industrial era when working conditions were often harsh, if not downright dangerous, and a job was not necessarily interesting or fulfilling. Our values have evolved. People today look for work that is not only remunerative but rewarding as well. One thing is certain: If we truly recognized the social, moral and spiritual dimension of work, we would be doing more to educate young people; we would be making a greater effort to help them integrate into the labour market; we would take it for granted that, in order for young people to lead successful lives, no effort should be spared to enable them to actively participate in society.

That was the principle that guided me. Although it can be said that we had moved things forward a little, we were still a long way from the ultimate goal. As for the two pilot projects that our efforts produced, the one in New-Brunswick bore fruit because Premier McKenna believed in it and cared about it. The one in Newfoundland was an example of a project that had been offered but not invited, and toward which the provincial government was not particularly committed. Therefore, it did not achieve the kind of success I had hoped for in that province. Nevertheless, once the pilot projects were put in place, other provinces, suddenly realizing they had passed up a promising opportunity, expressed an interest in joining the program. But it was too late—the money had been spent. The 1988 elections intervened, and I did not, in the end, achieve the essence of what I was aiming for, which was a major overhaul of Unemployment Insurance legislation. To this day, Employment Insurance, as it is now called, and Welfare effectively stigmatize young people who are receiving benefits. Too often, these programs only confirm failure at a time in their lives when young people need to be given every opportunity to succeed.

The Ben Johnson Affair

In the spring of 1988 Michou gave birth to Antoine, our second child. A few days later the Prime Minister shuffled his Cabinet and entrusted me with the added responsibility of Amateur Sport. This Cabinet shuffle also brought Lucien Bouchard to Ottawa from Paris where he had been serving as Canada's ambassador to France. I met him for the first time at Rideau Hall, where I was sworn in as Minister for Youth and Amateur Sport.

Although I, personally, was not very athletic, I was taking over the portfolio from Otto Jelinek who had been very popular with sporting groups, he being a former world champion figure skater. The Winter Olympics had just been held in Calgary and had been a great success for that city and for Canada. I was arriving on the job a little like a dog in a game of ninepins, to paraphrase a French expression. It should be noted that the world of amateur sport in Canada is very small. In addition, it presents a faithful reflection of society at large. It mirrors all the tensions that arise in Canadian society. At every major national and international event, for example, the language question surfaces. Nothing is more typical of the Canadian amateur sporting environment. It is also an environment that is very "politicized" in the sense that an awful lot goes on behind the scenes. For someone who is not from that environment and not familiar with it, the learning curve is steep.

I took office a few months before the Seoul Olympic Games, close on the heels of a new policy initiative, championed by my predecessor Otto Jelinek, to combat the use of performance-enhancing drugs in amateur sports. At the time, Canada was organizing an international conference on "doping" in sport, which was to be held in Ottawa. As minister, the first decision I had to make was whether or not to pursue the idea of holding the conference. By doing so, Canada agreed to take on a leadership role on the basis of its position with regard to sanctions put forth by Jelinek. The sanction process was predicated on a suspension for life, at the first infraction, for any athlete found to be using a performance-enhancing drug. My initial reaction to such a scenario was very negative. I told my deputy that in criminal law a life-sentence is as close to God as you can get, and that I had strong reservations about imposing that kind of sanction. He explained to me that Canada, in the person of Otto Jelinek, had already taken on a leading role on the issue. As we were organizing an international conference for the purpose of proposing uniform rules, we had to set the standard very high in order to be in a position to readjust it during the course of negotiations, depending on the consensus that would emerge.

After thinking long and hard about the matter, I finally accepted his arguments and made them my own. The conference in question took place just before the Seoul Olympics. Different countries suggested standards. We did not change ours because the discussions on sanctions had not advanced beyond the preliminaries. Therefore, at the time of the Seoul Olympics, the sanction of suspension for life was still, officially, part of the administrative standards of Sport Canada. It meant that the government of Canada would deny, for life, funding to any athlete found guilty of a doping infraction.

A few weeks before the Olympic Games, the first incident took place. I was in my Sherbrooke riding when I received a phone call from Ottawa informing me that some Canadian weight-lifters from Québec had been tested while in transit to Seoul, and that traces of an anabolic steroid had been found in their urine. I was reminded that established administrative policy dictated an automatic lifetime suspension. This was not a pleasant decision to make, especially as it applied to young people who were on the verge of fulfilling their dream of taking part in the Olympic Games. Nevertheless, the policy of my department was clear and unequivocal. As the minister, I had to apply it. I suspended the weight-lifters. The department put out a press release. It caused nary a ripple in the public and seemed to elicit only indifference in sporting circles. But, I was soon to discover, there is a hierarchy in the world of amateur sport, and weight-lifters, for example, are not perceived as being in the same league as 100-metre runners. So the incident had gone practically unnoticed.

By the time the Seoul Olympics began, the election was literally around the corner. I was anxious about my own re-election in Sherbrooke. I was taking nothing for granted. I was eager to return to my riding. Add to that the fact that Antoine, our baby, was only a few months old. I had already decided that I would not attend the Games when the Prime Minister's Office contacted me. They wanted me to make the trip. From their perspective, it was important for the government of Canada to be there. Canadians care about the Olympic Games. It is a unifying event for the whole country. I was reminded that we were on the eve of an election; our absence from Seoul would send the wrong message.

In the end, I reluctantly agreed to go, but only for four days. Michou accompanied me. We attended the opening ceremonies. We had some important meetings. Among others, I met with Juan Antonio Samaranch, the President of the International Olympic Committee, to take up the issue of integrating sports for the physically disabled into the Olympic Games. Samaranch showed little interest. In Canada, by contrast, sports for the physically disabled have been popularized by people like the late Terry Fox, Sherbrooke-born André Viger, and Rick Hanson. Canadians support and admire these disabled athletes mainly because they personify the Olympic spirit as defined by Pierre de Coubertin. These athletes remind us that the competition that truly matters is the one that takes place within the heart and mind of each athlete to achieve his or her own personal best; that the struggle to excel, to push back one's own limits is probably the most fulfilling of all—physically as well as spiritually. However, the Olympic Games, mirroring professional sport, have become commercialized. This may be seen as inevitable, and may, in itself, be neither good nor bad. But it does have consequences in terms of shaping attitudes about amateur sport. Victory has become a supreme, if not the only, value to be sought by any means necessary and at any price.

Michou and I returned home at the end of a long trip. The night of the 100-metre race, Ben Johnson beat the world record, won the gold, and the whole country went wild. The next morning, Canadians were in shock. They learned that a test had revealed the presence of stenosolol, an anabolic steroid, in Johnson's urine. I was informed of the matter in the middle of the night, barely a few hours before the news exploded like a bomb in the media. Beyond my own consternation over what had just happened, I was faced with a dilemma. I had just suspended four weight-lifters for the same infraction a few weeks earlier. I could not apply the sanction differently to Johnson. In the meantime, the IOC confirmed the verdict, stripped Johnson of his gold medal, and suspended him.

I had to announce my decision, and my lack of experience showed. Rather than wait a few days and take the time to explain the why's and wherefore's of Sport Canada's policy on sanctions before applying it, I wanted to be consistent and avoid creating a double-standard. Therefore, I applied the exact same sanction to Ben Johnson as I had to the weight-lifters. The problem was that the latter incident had gone practically unnoticed by the public. In the Johnson case there was an instant storm of protest, amid which my colleague, Jelinek, came out and declared publicly that the life sanction was too severe. I could not believe it. Obviously the sanction I had announced was perceived as neither fair nor equitable in the eyes of most Canadians. Meanwhile, the confusion only grew. It was learned that Ben Johnson and his trainer protested their innocence. The whole thing became an unbelievable media circus. My colleagues in the caucus, acutely aware that an election was imminent, were appalled. Finally, the government decided to set up a Royal Commission of inquiry, chaired by Justice Charles Dubin, into doping in sport, to try to get to the bottom of things. It was later to produce an historic report, whose recommendations honoured Canada and made a decisive impact on the attitudes of governments and sports groups around the world with regard to the use of performance-enhancing drugs in sport.

True Valour

At this juncture, Prime Minister Mulroney called a general election. As they say, to be elected is one thing, to be re-elected is another. For all those who, in a first election, coast into office on the crest of a wave, the merit is not as great as it is when they face the electorate for the second time and are given a second mandate on the basis of their record. The election in Sherbrooke was hotly contested. I faced a strong opponent in Dennis Wood, a well-known Sherbrooke business man. The day after the leaders' debate, in which John Turner performed beyond expectations and scored some telling blows against Mulroney on the crucial question of Canada-U.S. Free Trade, public opinion polls showed a sharp rise in Liberal support, and we began to worry in earnest. That was when Mulroney showed his strength of character. The real test in politics is not when everything is going your way, but when you stumble. Mulroney got back on his feet, grabbed the bull by the horns, and won the election. That being said, the campaign left us badly injured with long term damage in Ontario, the West, and the Atlantic region.

Once re-elected, Prime Minister Mulroney reconfirmed me as Minister of State for Youth and Amateur Sport, with the added responsibility of becoming Deputy

House Leader. This new role necessitated my almost constant presence in the House of Commons, whereas my ministerial responsibilities required that I travel extensively within Canada and abroad. As Minister for Sport, for example, I participated in the founding and preparation of the first Games of the Francophonie, which were held in Morocco in 1989. I had to travel to Morocco several times in preparation for the Games. We also had to negotiate the participation in these Games of the three governments involved, i.e. the governments of Canada, Québec, and New-Brunswick. Negotiations were arduous, particularly with my Québec counterpart, Yvon Picotte, whom I got to know better later on. I was also the first chairman of the International Committee for these Games, which gave me an opportunity to familiarize myself with the international institutions of the Francophonie and North-South institutions. When the Francophone Games were created, we introduced two important elements: sports for the physically disabled and an obligation to alternate the Games' site between countries of the North and of the South. The aim was to ensure that the Games would be held in developing countries. Sport is too often the preserve of wealthy countries that have the financial means to sponsor the careers of top athletes and can afford to put on a show of spectacular dimensions. It is because sport has a moral, humanitarian and unifying role to play in society that we insisted that the Games alternate between North and South and that countries be allowed to hold the Games in accordance with what each could afford. There was no question of setting a grandiose standard that would apply equally to all. Instead, the point was to develop access to the international sporting arena for athletes from the francophone world. Also, we decided to include a very important cultural dimension in the Francophone Games to distinguish them from all other International competitions.

The other priority objective I pursued as Minister for Sport was the introduction of athletics for the physically disabled into the Canada Games. Our proposal had been well received by provincial ministers. At the Summer Games in Saskatoon in 1989, the Canadian Ministers of Sport unanimously decided to include competitions for the physically disabled in our next hosting of the Canada Games and all others thereafter. With this accomplished, we immediately changed target and set our sights on the Commonwealth Games of 1994, which were to be held in Victoria, British Columbia. I had already made the case to the Commonwealth Games Association in 1988 at the Seoul Olympics. I made it again in 1990 at the Commonwealth Games in Auckland, New Zealand. In both cases my proposal was politely, but categorically, rejected. Nevertheless, I was delighted when sports for the physically disabled were integrated into the Commonwealth Games: first as a pilot project in Victoria in 1994, and then fully and officially thereafter.

My ultimate objective was to persuade the Olympic Committee to confer as much value and prestige on the medals won by physically disabled athletes as on all the others. Much remains to be done in this respect. To this day, the two sets of events are held separately. There are the Olympics, for the "real athletes", and the Special Olympics for the physically disabled who do not receive the same medals and do not climb onto the same podiums. By acting in this manner, we tell those young people that their medals, that their efforts, do not have the same worth as those of "real athletes", whereas the very opposite is true. I was not advocating that all sports for the physically disabled be integrated in the Olympic Games, only that certain sports be included, and that the medals be the same for everyone. We have not arrived at that point yet, but inevitably, we will—just as women's hockey came to be part of the Olympics. In this respect, sport is a true mirror of society.

Stay in School

In addition to my responsibilities as Deputy House Leader and Minister for Amateur Sport, I had to decide how to follow up on the efforts I made as Minister for Youth during the first mandate of the government. The comprehensive policy initiative to which I had devoted so much energy was still not a priority for the government. Therefore, I sought to implement my Youth Policy on a piecemeal basis. We decided to concentrate on the pressing problem of school drop-outs. I engaged in a new round of consultations with educators across the country. Canada, then as now, particularly when compared to other industrialized countries, suffered from an alarming school drop-out rate. Once again, this was partly the result of the fact that Canada's economy was undergoing a painful transition to a post-industrial economy based on human, rather than purely natural, resources—a change to what we now call a knowledge-based economy. Canada had not done enough to prepare itself for such a transition, whereas the world all around us was changing at an unprecedented rate to keep pace with the ever-expanding phenomenon of globalization.

Our policy focused on a major effort to encourage young people to stay in school or training. Too often, young people who experience failure very early in life psychologically remain with failure for the rest of their days. The message they get from that experience is that they cannot succeed. The experience of failure in the school system can undermine confidence in one's self for the future. In this regard, our consultations with educators were revealing. I particularly remember a meeting at the senior high-school level where someone said to me, "Mr. Charest, what you are proposing is fine for kids aged fifteen to sixteen. It's important, but it is very late in the process. If you really want to help potential drop-outs, you have to start much earlier than that. A good first or second grade teacher is probably able to tell you which of his or her students will have problems once they reach high-school." In short, if we really wanted to do something about the drop-out problem, we had to do it much earlier in a young person's education. I decided to further investigate the matter. I went to the United States to meet with the Secretary of State for Education in the Reagan administration. He described the Head Start program that had addressed the drop-out problem in the ghettoes of America with some success. The American Secretary of State did not mince his words: "You have to start with the parents", he said. "You have to get to young mothers practically from the moment they are pregnant. That's when it all starts." The drop-out problem is indeed a matter for parents as much as for their children. We had come to the same conclusion ourselves in 1987 while preparing a $200 million anti-drug strategy: The primary influence on children is the example their parents set for them.

With this in mind, we got to work on preparing a policy called Stay in School. It had several aspects: one provided community-based support; another provided support within the school system; and a third was a summer jobs program that offered training and work experience to potential drop-outs. The aim was to motivate the students to stay in school by making them aware of the alternatives available and by familiarizing them with the world of work. The purpose was to restore their sense of worth by showing them their true potential. Our approach was based on the principle that these young people, for one reason or another, had lost confidence in themselves and needed help to rebuild their confidence and identify the choices before them. In essence, the message was: If you decide to leave school, this is what you can expect; if you choose to continue with your education, these are the opportunities that will be open to you. You decide. In some cases, they still decided to drop out, but did so in full knowledge of the probable consequences. More often, however, a change was evident in the young people who had recovered their self-confidence, and a moving scene commonly resulted. At the end of the program, there was a graduation ceremony. Families were invited. For the young people involved, it was often the first time in their lives that an achievement of theirs had been formally recognized. It was exciting, like the first time a kid puts the ball in the basket or scores a goal in hockey. Everyone is watching. Everyone cheers. For the youths involved, this kind of experience confirms and reinforces the feeling that he or she is capable of success.

Looking back, the Stay in School program was one of the most personally satisfying achievements of my political life. I had consulted provincial Ministers of Education, including Claude Ryan, then Québec Minister of Education. At first, some of them expressed reluctance because education is a provincial jurisdiction. But, in the end, the program proved its worth and all the provinces came onboard. The program even became a priority for the Government of Québec. One of my Cabinet colleagues, namely Lucien Bouchard, was a strong supporter of the new program. Sadly, it was dropped by the Federal government after the 1993 election.

Life Goes On

In January, 1990 I was in Auckland, New-Zealand attending the Commonwealth Games, mainly for the purpose of promoting the inclusion of sports for physically disabled athletes in the Games and getting agreement on a pilot project for them at the 1994 Games in Victoria. We were then in the midst of a controversy over language that is sadly typical of major sporting events in Canada. A young Québec athlete named Michel Brodeur, who had participated in the trials prior to the Auckland Games, had been excluded from the Canadian team. His performance, while achieving the international standard for participation in the Games, did not meet the higher Canadian standard. The purpose of setting a higher standard was to assemble the best possible team and to limit its size, as Canadian teams in the past had acquired a reputation for being too large. That, however, was not my concern. My main preoccupation was to ensure that our teams reflected the make-up of our country, and, therefore, included a proportion of francophone athletes. The obsession with standards displayed by the Canadian Team seemed, to me, to contradict the ideal embodied by the Games. I believe they exist to enable those who qualify to have the opportunity to surpass themselves in the context of a moment that is unique in their lives. Is that not precisely the purpose of international competitions of this kind? Should they not ensure the participation of young athletes who not only meet the established standards but are capable of surpassing them beyond all expectations at the time of the actual event? Why limit ourselves to only the very top athletes, thereby excluding the possibility of unanticipated victories? Why stifle a degree of spontaneity and unpredictability in favour of an obsession with performance?

At the same time, another Québecer, a coach named Daniel Saint-Hilaire, was in court in Montreal trying to reverse the decision to exclude him from the Canadian Team. In Auckland, I apprised the representatives of the Canadian Commonwealth Games Association of my concerns. I had a letter sent to Daniel Saint-Hilaire's lawyer reiterating the substance of the assurances I had obtained from the representatives of the Canadian Commonwealth Games Association. In essence, it said that if the court rendered a decision in favour of Michel Brodeur, they would comply with it, given that the Games were about to begin. My letter was produced in court. Confusion ensued. In the midst of it all, I made the mistake of concluding, from what my assistants were telling me, that I was to call the judge in the case to clarify the content of my letter. Even though I was a lawyer by training, and understood perfectly well the nature of the relationship between the legislative and judiciary, I spontaneously agreed to call the judge. As soon as I had him on the line, I said, "I understand you wish me to clarify the content of my letter." He answered, "No". The conversation ended then and there. Nevertheless, I was a Minister of the Crown. The simple fact that I had placed the call carried the supreme sanction. I gave my resignation to the Prime Minister thinking I had just ended my political career and ruined everything. My wife Michou was with me. I was devastated by the thought of what this was doing to her, my family, friends and colleagues,.

What followed was extremely painful, but very heartening. In Sherbrooke, the incident prompted a wave of sympathy that moved me very deeply. People there understood that there had been no attempt on my part to influence a judge. They knew that I had not acted in my own personal interest. On the way home, Michou and I made a stopover in the Fiji islands to recover our strength and prepare to face the music. When you resign, the fall is brutal. When you resign from the Cabinet, the department calls your office on the Hill to reclaim the furniture. On a human level, it is painful and humiliating.

When we returned to Canada, however, we were very grateful to find a busload of supporters from Sherbrooke waiting for us at the airport. They had come to say they still had confidence in me. I spoke to my father to apologize for the embarrassment I had caused him and he said, "Don't. I know you'll get back on your feet." We attended a reception in Montreal given by our Sherbrooke supporters. Then we went and spent a few hours with my in-laws and my own family. After that, we headed for Ottawa to be with our children, the youngest of whom, Alexandra, had been born the previous November. The next day, when I went into the weekly meeting of our caucus, I remembered what my mother always used to tell me: life goes on; what counts is to get back on your feet. I already knew what I was going to do. I got up, I apologized to my colleagues for the trouble I had caused them and then repeated that I was there to work and to do my part.

I went back to the House of Commons the same day. In those circumstances, it is a solemn moment. As a Minister, I had been sitting in the front benches of the House. Now my seat was somewhere at the back, close to the curtains. Everything around me physically reminded me of the change in my status. I had seen the procession of other ministers who had been obliged to resign before me. The first time you enter the House for Question Period, there is complete silence. Everyone observes the ritual. For you, it is a long march. I walked to my seat. I sat down, and heaved a sigh of relief. I thought, "That's it, then. It's done. Life goes on."

I thought I had thrown everything away, but, strangely, the period that followed was one of the happiest of our lives. I was then thirty-one years old. We had just been blessed with our third child. Antoine was still very young, as was Amélie. Our children needed a lot of attention. I had devoted much time and energy to my work in recent years. All of a sudden, we were able to enjoy a period of calm, to be alone together, the five of us. I was able to spend some time with my family. We could slow down and see our friends. I was less in the public eye. We spent more time in the Eastern Townships. I finally had time to enjoy life and devote myself to the things that matter in life. I realized how much my work as a Minister had consumed me. But this period of calm didn't last long…

The Country had Changed

When the Prime Minister first appointed me to his Cabinet in 1986, he also asked me to sit on a Cabinet committee whose mandate was to prepare constitutional negotiations on Canadian Unity. The purpose of those negotiations was to get Québec to sign the 1982 Constitution Act. As I had a long-standing interest in the subject, I was both pleased and flattered to have been given this responsibility. Lowell Murray, then government leader in the Senate and Minister of Intergovernmental Affairs, chaired the committee. Also sitting on the committee were Joe Clark, Jake Epp, Marcel Masse, Benoît Bouchard, Gerry Weiner, and Senator Arthur Tremblay, himself an institution, a father of the Quiet Revolution and for many years a top Québec civil servant.

Our mandate was to prepare the ground work for a meeting, which was later to take place at Meech Lake, between Prime Minister Mulroney and the provincial Premiers. From the outset, the committee clearly stated that we could not contemplate such negotiations unless the chances of success were extremely high. We were not going to risk engaging the government in a debate that would consume all the country's energies, as had been the case in 1981-82, without first ensuring success. In other words, we were then well aware that this debate was not like all the others; it would require a costly investment in time and energy, and it was not a process one launched without careful preparation.

These internal discussions were taking place on the basis of a speech that Brian Mulroney gave in Sept-Îles during the 1984 election campaign, which, by the way, did not constitute a major plank of his platform. The Sept-Îles speech, in which Brian Mulroney pledged to bring Québec back into the Canadian constitutional fold "with honour and enthusiasm," is presented by some today as having been the turning point of the 1984 campaign in Québec. Nothing could be further from the truth. The outcome had already been decided. Mulroney's speech was important, but, in terms of the methodology involved, there were a certain number of steps that had to be undertaken before we got to the stage of proposing constitutional amendments.

First, the political will to make changes had to be expressed. Mulroney did that in his speech. Next, a response was needed. Finally, before any amendment is proposed, a consensus is required. Mulroney outlined the problem he wanted to solve during the 1984 campaign, but not how he planned to do it. He gave no details. It would have been neither timely nor appropriate for him to have done so. The response came in 1985 from the newly elected government of Robert Bourassa, who did not then make a major campaign pledge out of the issue any more than we did in 1984. In a speech at Mont Gabriel, near Montreal, Québec Minister Gil Rémillard outlined the six conditions for Québec to sign the 1982 Constitution Act. Ultimately, an agreement on starting a new round of constitutional negotiations, based on the principles put forward by the government of Québec, was reached at the provincial Premiers' conference in Edmonton in August, 1986.

The Edmonton Conference was preceded by a series
of exchanges and an effort at orchestration in which I did
not participate and of which I had no knowledge. This was
also the case for the great majority of my ministerial
colleagues—for good reason. Such an initiative must be
meticulously planned. It cannot be improvised. It is too
important in the life of a country. In this case, it was done in
a straightforward manner and all the pieces fell into place.

The third step was reached when we obtained a
consensus. From a methodological point of view, this is
very important. We now had an agenda with which to
begin a discussion. It included Rémillard's declarations
and added certain concerns of the Western provinces.
Alberta Premier Don Getty, who chaired the Edmonton
meeting, requested that Senate Reform be included in the
agenda for future talks. Brian Peckford, the Premier of
Newfoundland, insisted that the issue of Management of
the Fisheries, no surprise, be included as well. This was all
part of the normal course of affairs. The main thing was
that Québec's terms for acceptance of the 1982 Constitution
Act were discussed.

As a follow-up to the Edmonton conference, and in
anticipation of formal negotiations between all of the
country's First Ministers, the Cabinet Committee, of which
I was a member, took up the task of preparing the federal
position during the summer of 1986. This was a fascinating
experience for me. Our mission was to offer the Prime
Minister a thorough analysis, and a winning scenario for
the country, while defining the federal interest as clearly as
possible. With these recommendations in hand, the Prime
Minister chaired the now famous First Ministers' meeting
that was held at Meech Lake, and which, to everyone's
surprise, produced an agreement. A 'window' had opened,
such as happens only rarely in a country's history, and all
efforts had combined to make the negotiation a success.
At the time, most observers were astonished.

In the month that followed, the agreement was the subject of much vigorous, but not heated, debate. If concerns were raised, they gave us no reason to foresee trouble. Therefore, the First Ministers met again, in Ottawa, in the Langevin Block where the Prime Minister's office is located, to finalize the legal text of the agreement. That meeting, which lasted far into the night, also produced agreement. Once again, observers could not believe their eyes.

Then began what has been called the Meech Lake Saga. First came an election in New Brunswick that swept Premier Hatfield's government from office and brought to power a new Liberal government under a new Premier named Frank McKenna. McKenna had not been a party to the Meech Lake negotiations and had naïvely pledged not to follow up on the accord negotiated by his predecessor. Shortly thereafter, the Québec government decided to invoke the notwithstanding clause in reaction to the Supreme Court judgment on the Québec sign law. This, in turn, prompted a reaction in Manitoba, where Gary Filmon's minority government was fighting for survival against two opposition parties who were both fiercely opposed to the Meech Lake Accord. Faced with a storm of protest in his province over the Québec government's actions, Filmon withdrew his support for Meech. We were losing control of the situation. Now the problem was serious.

What was remarkable about this period was that the country had changed. Up until then, First Ministers' negotiations had always been conducted behind closed doors and the outcome announced to the people. What no one had fully understood was that ever since patriation of the Canadian Constitution and the adoption of the Charter of Rights and Freedoms, many groups of citizens had come to identify closely with the Charter. Canadians, in general, identified more closely with the Constitution of their country. Not only did they feel directly concerned by the constitutional amendments we were proposing, but, to a certain extent, they felt excluded from them. They insisted that their interests and opinions be taken into account. Across the country, women's groups, francophones from outside Québec, Québec anglophones, ethnic minorities and, above all, the Aboriginal peoples of Canada demanded a say in the process of change.

The Aboriginal side of this story deserves further mention. Aboriginal opposition to the Accord was gaining momentum, especially in view of the fact that the Meech Lake agreement had been reached in the aftermath of the 1987 Constitutional Conference on the rights of Aboriginal peoples, which had ended in failure and had increased the level of Aboriginal frustration by several orders of magnitude. What we were then experiencing in Canada, without fully realizing it at the time, was the beginning of a period of affirmation for Aboriginal peoples. Movements of this kind often emerge around a symbolic event. Unfortunately, for those who believed in it, the Meech Lake Accord became a symbol of exclusion for Aboriginal peoples.

All these elements combined meant that the context in which we were proposing new constitutional amendments had radically changed. At the time of patriation in 1981-82, there had been no call for a referendum to approve constitutional changes. Now the people demanded direct participation in constitutional decision-making. Regardless, the Prime Minister and the Premiers proceeded, and, while doing so, failed to take sufficient notice of the opposition until it was too late. The thinking was that the situation was still manageable; McKenna's and Filmon's concerns could be addressed. Surely they would not go so far as to derail a process so vital to the future of Canada. Stormy weather was certainly upon us—but no one realized that we were in the path of a hurricane.

The Storm

To put the situation in perspective, you have to remember that when the Meech Lake Accord was signed in 1987, the mechanisms for constitutional change had been in place for only five years. We were putting them to the test for the first time. The first of these mechanisms, the 'general amending procedure', requires the approval of seven provinces including 50% of the population of Canada, with a deadline of one year for all of the country's legislatures to vote on the changes. The second mechanism sets a far more stringent standard and is used for changes requiring a much higher level of consent. This second amendment procedure requires unanimous approval of all the provinces and the Federal government. In addition to that, the advice which the First Ministers received was to apply the most stringent procedure, i.e. unanimity, with a deadline of three years. Consequently, they had a considerable period of time ahead of them to have the Accord approved in each of their legislatures. If everyone had been more aware of the political realities with which we were faced (Canada then was an anxious country, unsettled by profound economic and social change), it would have been understood that the "window" for proposing such major changes does not remain open very long. Unless the ratification process goes ahead almost immediately, the window inevitably closes. This is true in any democratic country that attempts to implement changes of this nature. If you leave such an initiative on the table for too long, it becomes the object of a political debate that goes well beyond the issues first addressed. This was not understood. Meech became a ship adrift in a sea of protest.

Aboriginal objections in particular could not be ignored. Territorial governments also had legitimate concerns. For example, the Accord provided for a provincial say in appointments to the Senate. The Territories are also represented in the Senate, but the Accord was silent on that score. In the eyes of Northerners, it was as though the leaders from central Canada, Ontario and Québec in particular, viewed this as an irrelevant detail, but, to them, it was symbolically very important. Responding to these concerns would have necessitated a simple amendment, a civilized gesture, that consisted of saying, "You have governments too, so you too should be consulted on the appointment of Senators representing your region." There was no valid reason not to do it. However, positions had hardened in the interim. In response, the government of Québec kept raising the stakes. In the hope of forcing the opponents of the Accord to give way, it adopted a steamroller approach that did not have the intended result. People with often legitimate objections to Meech only dug in more.

At the same time, in 1989, a new government came to power in Newfoundland, which was headed by a new premier, Clyde Wells. Not only had he not participated in the Meech Lake negotiations, but he gave himself the mission of fighting the Accord. His position was both dogmatic and intransigent.

In 1988, Lucien Bouchard, though unelected, was appointed to the Cabinet. He was previously stationed in Paris as Canada's Ambassador to France. He was also

named Québec lieutenant, i.e. Québec caucus leader and
Prime Minister Mulroney's trusted right-hand man in
Québec. This caused great excitement in the Québec
caucus because, up until then, we had not really had a
lieutenant. The position is very important politically,
though it carries no specific job-description. The main
qualification for the position is to have the confidence of
the leader. Everything else is secondary. Those who call
upon the lieutenant for help in advancing a particular file
have to know he has access to the leader of the government and that his opinions carry some weight. Before
Lucien Bouchard, the lieutenant was Marcel Masse, but
it was known that Masse did not have the ear of Brian
Mulroney. This was the situation when Lucien Bouchard
took up his duties inside the federal government.

After the 1988 election, which had been fought on
the highly controversial issue of Free Trade and had
prompted bitter, harrowing debates, the public discussion
that resumed around the Meech Lake Accord took an
alarming turn. The Québec government, continuously
urged on by the Parti Québécois whose objective it was to
scuttle the Accord, seemed more and more entrenched
and its positions more and more unalterable. The more
inflamed the rhetoric became, the harder it was to bring
people back to reason. One particularly unfortunate incident occurred at a joint press conference with a Minister
of the Québec government and Lucien Bouchard, who
suggested that if Newfoundland wasn't happy, it should
leave the Federation. Coming from a former diplomat,
that statement was anything but helpful. A man or woman
in the street is free to think what he or she likes, even to
say it, but when you accept responsibilities such as those
Lucien Bouchard had in a government that represents all
Canadians, you do not speak in only your name. You cannot
just indulge yourself. These statements caused an uproar
and greatly undermined the political will of the other

actors involved. At the same time, in the rest of the country, many were those who did not hesitate to try and score political points by opposing Meech, including Jean Chrétien who, in a speech at the University of Ottawa in January 1990, attacked the clause in the Accord that would have recognized Québec as a "distinct society" within Canada. According to him, the crux of the issue was whether or not the clause took precedence over the Charter of Rights and Freedoms, which is an emotional hot button for all those in Canada for whom the Charter is a powerful symbol. The full force and fury of the hurricane was now upon us.

"The Chairman Should be You"

In March, 1990, I was no longer in the Cabinet. I had resigned two months earlier. One Saturday night, Michou and I were invited to dinner at the home of Camille Guilbault, a friend who served as liaison between the caucus and the Prime Minister's Office. Also present at this dinner were Pierre Blais and his wife Chantal, and Lucien Bouchard and his wife Audrey Best, whom Michou had gotten to know as they had been pregnant at the same time. Meech at that time was a dying patient. The Premier of New Brunswick, Frank McKenna, had proposed a parallel accord to Meech, an approach inspired by American History (The Thirteen Colonies, when they were negotiating a constitutional agreement, had reached an impasse and, to break the deadlock, resorted to a parallel accord to preserve their initial agreement while addressing the concerns of those who had objections). This was a good way to respond to the many legitimate concerns of those who wanted to correct what they saw as serious oversights in the Meech Lake Accord and still ensure the Accord's survival.

Hoping to salvage Meech, the Prime Minister announced he was setting up a Special Committee of the

House of Commons to review the parallel accord
proposed by McKenna. The following Saturday, during the
dinner at Camille Guilbault's, Bouchard raised the
question of who should sit on the committee and said to
me, "The chairman should be you." I was surprised and a
little suspicious, for I knew that the risks associated with
such an enterprise were very high. I have many faults, but
naïveté is not one of them. At the same time, life for me
had taken a happy turn. Michou and I savoured the time
to ourselves that my freedom from Cabinet responsibilities
allowed us. Some that night saw Bouchard's proposal as an
opportunity for me to return to the Cabinet and prove
myself anew, but I was acutely aware of the risks involved
and was in no rush to accept such a mandate.

That evening, we discussed the substance of the
McKenna proposal. One of the concerns at the root of
McKenna's initial opposition to the Meech Lake Accord
was the contentious issue of the promotion of Canada's
linguistic duality. McKenna approached that question
from the perspective of the Acadians, who make up one-
third of the population of his province. They wanted the
French language and culture promoted in their part of
New Brunswick. In their eyes, the Accord's silence on the
matter seemed to say that their concerns were being
minimized. McKenna had taken up their cause and the
parallel accord he was proposing reflected that.

As it happens, the Senator and constitutional scholar
Gérald Beaudoin had published an article in the newspaper Le Devoir that very day. In it, he stated that McKenna's
proposal was no cause for concern as it suggested promoting linguistic duality only in the federal government's
fields of jurisdiction. This, then, had no impact on
provincial fields of jurisdiction and none, therefore, on
the Charter of the French Language. During the
discussion we had at the dinner table that night, I told
Bouchard that I concurred with Senator Beaudoin's

analysis, and that I interpreted what McKenna was proposing in the same way.

Two days later, Lucien and I had another conversation. According to my brother, who worked for him as an aide, Lucien was very much in favour of my chairing the Committee. At the same time he was considering who else, in the Québec caucus, should sit on the Committee, which was to include fifteen members. It was therefore very important to chose M.P.s who were representative, solid and credible. We discussed names before I even accepted his offer to chair. Lucien sent me a note on the subject during Question Period suggesting the names of André Plourde and Gabriel Desjardins. In the end, at his request and mine, these two M.P.s were selected to join the Committee.

I received a call from Prime Minister Mulroney later the same afternoon. He asked to see me. I went to his office where he asked me to chair the Committee. I had had time to think about it and accepted, with reservations. I told him I would do my utmost, but that I needed the government to support me because I expected the Committee hearings to be fraught with controversy and the Committee itself to be attacked from all sides. I received numerous assurances, from Bouchard and Mulroney, to the effect that they would support me in my efforts. Nevertheless, the Committee began its work under a dark cloud. We had a dying patient in Meech. My objective was to revive the patient so the First Ministers could take over. The aim was not to find THE solution, but rather to draw up a menu from which the first ministers would be able to chose solutions that seemed appropriate to them.

The Charest Committee

When I agreed to chair the Special Committee, two Senators who were members of our caucus, Gérald Beaudoin and Solange Chaput-Rolland, approached me to say that they would be willing to meet with me, advise me and give me an idea of what I could expect. Both had sat on the Pépin-Robarts Commission, which had been set up in 1977 by the Trudeau government after the 1976 election that brought René Lévesque and his Parti Québecois to power. That experience had taught them some lessons they wished to share with me. I immediately accepted their offer. They came to see me at my office. "You need to prepare yourself," they warned. "This kind of public consultation often attracts discontented, angry people who are going to say some very harsh things. This creates a very difficult work environment."

When the Committee first met, it became obvious that we were not going to be able to produce a unanimous report. The composition of the Committee almost guaranteed differing views. It included Liberals André Ouellet, Robert Kaplan, Bill Rompkey and Ethel Blondin, an Aboriginal M.P. from the Northwest Territories who took Aboriginal issues very much to heart, and New Democrats Svend Robinson and Lorne Nystrom. We all recognized the urgent need for action. One of our first decisions was to hold hearings not just in Ottawa but in regions of Canada where opposition to the Meech Lake Accord was strongest, i. e. the Northwest Territories, the Yukon, British Columbia, Manitoba and Newfoundland. We agreed that the Committee hearings should be televised. This had never been done before in the case of a committee that was to travel across the country.

The public hearings began in Ottawa. Frank McKenna was first to appear before the Committee since his government had originated the parallel accord we were mandated to review. The atmosphere in the Committee room was very tense. We knew we were under close media scrutiny. There were a whole series of testimonies by senior federal civil servants. Finally, it was the turn of the Premier of Ontario, David Peterson, to testify. After the opening hearings we flew aboard a Canadian Forces plane to Yellowknife. When we got there we were in for a shock. Bill Erasmus, an Aboriginal leader and the brother of George Erasmus (who would later co-chair the Royal Commission on Aboriginal Peoples) gave testimony that greatly dismayed us. He could not have cared less, he said, if Meech failed. It had nothing to do with the Aboriginal peoples he represented. That such a failure might have dire consequences for the future of Canada did not seem to trouble him in the least, quite the contrary. "It's your country," he said, "not ours." I was deeply troubled by his extremely negative views, not only on Meech, but also on relations between Aboriginals and other Canadians, and on the future of those relations. It was like hitting a wall. I felt very discouraged. His assessment left no possible way out. Later, in the plane that took us to the Yukon, one of my colleagues, Pauline Browse, who was later to become my junior Minister for the Environment, had all the other members of the committee sign a card which she gave to me to try to boost my morale.

Once we arrived in the Yukon, the tone of the hearings changed. We heard the testimony of Tony Penikett, the leader of the Yukon government and a New Democrat, whose position was constructive and who expressed a genuine willingness to find solutions that would enable Meech to survive while taking into account the concerns of the people of the North. The objections he expressed were moderate and reasonable. For instance, he stated that if Meech provided that provincial governments should be consulted regarding the appointment of Senators representing their province (one of Québec's conditions for signing onto Meech), then the same rule should apply to the governments of the Territories. Such a concern might seem unimportant to people from outside the North, but it reflected a widespread feeling among Northerners that they were being treated as second-class citizens. It was a point of view that seemed to me very sensible, but that was becoming more and more difficult to advocate because governments on both sides of the issue were becoming increasingly polarized. The Parti Québecois, which had everything to gain if Meech failed, was pushing the Bourassa government relentlessly on all those questions. "No compromise will be tolerated!" they cried. It was all or nothing at all! This inflexible attitude flew in the face of common sense, especially with regard to changes that had no impact on Québec's interests.

When we reached British Columbia, I remembered the words of Gérald Beaudoin and Solange Chaput-Rolland. We rented a hall in a well-known Vancouver hotel. The hearings were set to begin at nine o'clock in the morning. It was a beautiful day. People were in a good mood. When I arrived in the hearing room there were already several television cameras set up and ready to roll. The clerk informed me that Gordon Wilson, the leader of the Liberal Party of British Columbia, insisted on appearing before the Committee. However, the list of people demanding to be heard was endless. Although we had decided at the outset to hear government leaders, our time constraints were such (the Committee was to submit a report by mid-May, i.e. less than a month later) that it would have been impossible for us to hear the leaders of all of the country's opposition parties. We therefore decided to hear none, especially in view of the fact that they already had in their respective legislatures a forum in which to express their opinions publicly. As Gordon Wilson was the leader of an opposition party, he was told that he could not appear. He refused to accept this. As politics is done differently in British Columbia, he decided to manifest his displeasure at the opening of the Committee hearings in his province. He did so by forcing open the doors of the hearing room, with a horde of reporters television cameras in tow, demanding to be heard. He marched up to the table where we sat and began haranguing me and shouting insults. My colleagues and I were astonished at the spectacle Wilson was making of himself. Such antics, coming from the leader of a political party, were utterly irresponsible. It was a transparent attempt at media manipulation, and it got the day off to a very bad start. After that, it was going to be very difficult to restore order and have a substantive discussion on the issues.

The day was indeed long and difficult. Some people had constructive, even moving contributions to make. Others denounced us out of hand without offering the slightest hint of a suggestion that could have helped the country. According to the formula we had agreed upon, we were to hear experts, academics, business representatives, government leaders and Aboriginal leaders during the day. In addition, we reserved some time at the end of each day to accommodate a number of private citizens who wanted to be heard, providing they had submitted a written brief. The time allotted for each person was five minutes. This was very little, but it at least allowed people to have their say and it seemed to us the fairest, most inclusive way we could find to try and hear as many people as possible. At the end of that particularly trying day, we began hearing individuals; it was a nightmare. At the beginning of each testimony, when I would remind the persons before me they had only five minutes, their pent-up anger would explode. They would shout and hurl abuse. For a part of the public, at least the hearings were an opportunity to vent their frustrations. Some came to denounce the Canada-U.S. Free Trade Agreement. Every conceivable complaint against the government was aired that day.

With the hearings over in Vancouver, we flew to Winnipeg. The proceedings there lasted two and a half days. We were in for another shock. The hearing room was packed. For some reason that escapes me to this day, women's groups in Manitoba were at war with the Meech Lake Accord. I shall never forget the testimony of a young woman lawyer who was a spokesperson for a women's group opposed to Meech. She alleged that the clause recognizing Québec as a "distinct society" within Canada might some day be used by the Government of Québec to force women in that province to bear children, by out-lawing abortion, for the purpose of increasing the birth-rate. I remember the scene as if it were yesterday. There I was, sitting in my chair, saying to myself, "I'm dreaming. This can't be." I was staring at the young woman before me. She seemed quite normal. She was, after all, a lawyer. Nothing in her demeanour gave the slightest hint that she was capable of arriving at such an absurd conclusion. It was then that I realized how far the debate had degen-erated. What struck me most was not so much the fact that an individual could speak such nonsense, but that the hundred or so people in the room were all nodding their heads in agreement. The room was filled with perfectly reasonable, intelligent, educated people, many of them from academic circles, and yet they allowed themselves to get carried away to such an extent that they were able to listen to the most outrageous statements without uttering a word of protest.

This is but one example of the atmosphere in which the hearings were held and the perilous state to which public debate had fallen. It was worrisome, and it is useful to remind ourselves that it can happen. When it does, the men and women in the political arena have the responsibility of sounding the alarm and bringing everyone back to reason to keep the situation from degenerating further. In any case, we should never underestimate the possibility of this happening. In Canada we tend to be complacent about our own civility and believe debates of this kind cannot get out of hand as they so often do elsewhere. We think it cannot happen here. Unfortunately, this is simply not true. Anyone who witnessed the delirium of the Meech and post-Meech period will testify to that.

During our travels I got to know and appreciate Ethel Blondin, an Aboriginal (Liberal) M.P. from the Northwest Territories. She was both intelligent and naïve in the service of her ideals. We watched each other closely during the hearings. On Aboriginal issues, her reactions were a kind of barometer of what would be deemed acceptable or not, for she had voluntarily agreed to relay the positions of Aboriginal leaders to the Committee. One day in Vancouver, during a taxi ride between meetings, I said to her, "You know, Ethel, it would be tragic if Aboriginal peoples were to become the ultimate obstacle to final approval of the Meech Lake Accord. It would not be in their interest any more than it would be in the interest of Québecers. It would be tragic if we were to prevent each other from finding our rightful place in Canada." She looked at me and answered simply, "Jean, we can't. We can't wait any longer. We can't compromise any more."

There was also a unique political situation in Manitoba. Premier Gary Filmon's Conservative government was in a minority in the legislature and had no choice but to work closely with the two opposition parties. It was tightly wedged between the Liberals under Sharon Carstairs, a fierce opponent of Meech, and the New Democrats under Gary Doer, equally opposed to Meech, whose caucus included the Aboriginal M.L.A. Elijah Harper. In Manitoba, the Aboriginal leadership was totally mobilized against Meech. Aboriginal spokespersons (including Phil Fontaine and Ovide Mercredi) appeared nightly on national television, eloquently making their case against the Meech Lake Accord.

The Filmon government set up a provincial Commission of Inquiry chaired by Wally Fox-Decent. It held public hearings across Manitoba and produced a unanimous report proposing amendments to Meech, which in turn was endorsed by the provincial government. In the context of Manitoba, where the debate had degenerated to an extent I did not believe possible, this report had the advantage of presenting well-documented arguments in a formal framework. At the end of the day, during the period allotted to hear individual citizens, Izzy Asper, a well-known business leader, then current owner of Global Television, and a former leader of the Liberal Party of Manitoba, came before the Committee. As Chair, it was up to me to tell him he had only five minutes. When I did so, Mr. Asper became enraged. "What am I, chopped liver?" he stormed, to cheers and applause from the people in the hearing room.

After Manitoba, we headed to Newfoundland. The hearings in St. John's lasted a day and a half. The atmosphere was tense. One of the first witnesses to appear was the mayor of St. John's. His entire testimony was nothing but one long list of grievances against Québec, at the heart of which lay the contentious issue of the Churchill Falls hydroelectric contract[2]. What he was saying came down to this: If Québecers had treated us decently on Churchill Falls, we might be more open to Meech today. When he finished speaking, I asked him whether the Churchill Falls contract had anything to do with his position. He answered that it did not, but everything he said proved the opposite. I remembered what Gérald Beaudoin and Solange Chaput-Rolland had told me. The debate was degenerating into an inextricable tangle of recriminations that had nothing whatsoever to do with the Meech Lake Accord.

Next came the Premier of Newfoundland, Clyde Wells, flanked by his assistant Deborah Coyne. When I questioned Mr. Wells on the substance of his arguments against Meech, conflict erupted within the Committee itself. Labrador Liberal M.P. Bill Rompkey accused me of rudeness toward the Premier. Everything almost derailed at that moment. On the other hand we heard some very positive testimony, particularly from Craig Dobbin. He was then the owner of Canadian Helicopter and stood practically alone in his province in taking a position in favour of Meech. On that day, he expressed himself with courage and objectivity. Here was an influential business leader who had nothing to gain and everything to lose by expressing his views, which were contrary to the quasi-unanimous opinion of his fellow citizens in his province. But he insisted on doing so out of conviction and a sense of duty to his country.

---

[2] Churchill Falls hydroelectric contract: signed between the Churchill Falls Corporation (Labrador) and Hydro-Québec, on the construction and development of a hydroelectric dam on the Churchill River, in Labrador, for a duration of 65 years, and in which Newfoundlanders felt they had been "had" by Québec.

The Charest Report

We returned to Ottawa to begin our deliberations. While we were engaged in that work, I regularly informed Lucien Bouchard of developments, either directly or through my brother Robert. To me, Lucien Bouchard played a crucial role. As the Prime Minister's Québec lieutenant, it was up to him to rally members of the Cabinet and the caucus from Québec. The Québec ministers met for breakfast every Tuesday morning. The Québec caucus met on Tuesday evening, and on Wednesday morning there was a national caucus meeting. I relied on Lucien to inform our colleagues at the Québec ministers' breakfast to rally their support. On one occasion, I personally informed Lucien that the report would very probably contain a proposal to respond to Aboriginal concerns, to which he made no objection. On another, we discussed the matter of promoting linguistic duality, which he found difficult to accept and on which we disagreed.

The representatives of all three parties (Robert Kaplan for the Liberals, Lorne Nystrom for the New Democrats, and myself for the government) agreed on the need to submit a report that would be succinct and would present a range of options from which the First Ministers could choose. It was then that we realized we were going to be able to produce a unanimous report. We drew up a table of contents that I gave to Lucien. At the same time, I informed him of the content of the report we were drafting and asked him to relay the information to our colleagues from Québec. He assured me he would do so. He then announced, in response to a question from me, that he was going to be out of the country on the day the report would be made public—a date only ten days away!

I was dumbfounded. My brother Robert, who was a member of Bouchard's political staff, and who informed him daily of all developments regarding the drafting of the report, had not even been told. It was completely unexpected, and worrisome in the extreme. It was inconceivable to me that Lucien would be absent on that day and I told him so. I was not naïve. I told the Prime Minister in no uncertain terms that I would take one day after the report was made public to explain it to the media, but after that I would withdraw, for I knew very well that the report would live or die within the first twenty-four hours following its release. I also knew that if it died, Mulroney would be forced to distance himself from it as quickly as possible. The hard political reality was that his responsibility as Prime Minister of Canada went well beyond the work of one committee or of one Jean Charest, and his hands had to be free so he could do whatever was necessary to ensure Meech survived. That being said, in order to give the report every chance of being accepted by the public, the government had to defend it, and its chief spokesman on Québec all the more so. If Lucien Bouchard did not defend it, if he was not even present to defend it, the game was up before it even began. You did not have to be a genius to figure out what Jacques Parizeau, the leader of the Parti Québecois, would do on that day. His denunciation speech was already written, no matter what the report contained. There was nothing unexpected or mysterious about it. The script for his performance was a given: He was going to scream bloody murder and accuse us of high treason

Right after I had this conversation with Bouchard, I went up to my office and called the Prime Minister to tell him what had just been said. I repeated that Lucien absolutely had to be present for the report's release and if he was not it would send a very damaging signal. Mulroney and Bouchard, who were old friends, were to leave together that evening for Montreal, where they were to attend a commemorative event (related to the Cliche commission) at the Ritz-Carlton hotel. The Prime Minister assured me he would speak to Bouchard.

A few days later, Lucien left Canada to attend a conference on climatic change in Bergen, Norway. During this conference of environment ministers, he committed Canada, without previous authorization from the Cabinet, to reduce its emissions of greenhouse gases to the level of 1990 by the year 2000. It was an incredible gesture that instantly spread confusion and discord among his Cabinet colleagues and government departments and raised a storm of protest from Canadian business groups.

While Lucien was in Bergen, we faxed him successive drafts of our report to get feedback from him. He did not respond. Even worse, on May 17, the day the Report was to be made public, we learned that he was no longer in Bergen, the conference having ended, but in Paris where he had decided to take a few days' vacation with his family. I made repeated attempts to reach him in Paris, to no avail. He was, for all intents and purposes, incommunicado. After he insisted that I chair the committee, and without ever letting on that he harboured any serious reservations about the report we were preparing, he was now laying low, far from the heat of battle and impossible to reach. It was then that I realized there could no longer be any doubt about his true intentions. His absence had been carefully planned. On the 18th, as promised, I devoted a full day to giving interviews. I went to Montreal and met with the editorial board of *La Presse*. On Saturday, May 19, as I repeatedly called Paris in a fruitless attempt to reach him, Lucien launched his first missile in the form of a telegram of support to a meeting of the Parti Québécois in Alma, his home riding—a meeting to commemorate the tenth anniversary of the 1980 referendum on sovereignty-association. On Sunday, I was again unable to speak to Lucien as he was on a plane on his way back to Ottawa. Sensing that he was planning some dramatic gesture, I phoned Camille Guilbault in Ottawa to ask her to invite the other ministers from Québec to dinner at her house the following night. I then called each of them personally to relay the invitation.

It was a long week-end. On Monday, Michou, the children and I set out by car from the Eastern Townships to return to Ottawa. I spent the entire trip on my cell phone trying to reach Lucien at his office. Every time, he refused to take the call. Michou was at the wheel. She was furious. The babies were crying in the back. We arrived, finally. That afternoon, I went to the Hill, to Lucien's office, to try to meet with him. He refused to see me. I called Pierre Blais, who was very close to Lucien. Blais was devastated. He also tried to get in to see Lucien and finally succeeded late that afternoon. Their discussion was extremely painful. Lucien announced he was going to denounce the report and resign from the government.

Blais felt betrayed. So did I. Lucien had asked me to chair a committee whose mandate it was to draft recommendations for a parallel accord to the Meech Lake Accord. How could he claim to be surprised by the fact that our report contained proposals aimed at improving the Accord's chances of success? From the moment you accepted the idea of creating a committee to hear the objections of Meech opponents, it was obvious that it was going to submit recommendations that would address those objections, otherwise there would never have been a committee in the first place. It was self-evident. By denouncing the report, Lucien Bouchard was going to sign the Accord's death warrant.

The rest is history. The next day, Tuesday May 22, in an obviously calculated, premeditated gesture, and benefiting from unprecedented media hype, Lucien Bouchard dramatically resigned from the government. When I read his letter of resignation, I could not believe the lengths to which he was prepared to go in distorting the facts to suit his own purpose.

"It is with astonishment", he wrote, "that I learned, last week, in Europe, that this report proposes, as a basis for discussion at an eventual First Ministers' Conference, a list of some twenty-three modifications, several of which are changes that go to the heart of the conditions of the Accord." In the first place, what he was saying was not true. What the report contained were twenty-three recommendations, not modifications, two thirds of which did not even concern Québec's conditions. Secondly, he was kept faithfully informed, throughout the process, of the substance of the proposals about which he was today claiming to be so indignant. What was worse was that if, at the very end of the process, he had not been kept informed, it was indeed because he himself had seen to it that he could not be.

Meech Fails

I was in a state of shock. We all were. In Québec, only the PQ and its supporters celebrated. As for us, we had put our trust in Lucien. We had received no warning of the treachery he so meticulously planned. I recalled the Québec caucus meeting that had taken place, at Meech Lake of all places, the previous March, just before the government announced the creation of the Special Committee on the parallel accord. The discussion that day had been very intense and very emotional. Bouchard, having listened closely to everyone, concluded the meeting by saying, "First we have to give Mulroney every possible chance of salvaging Meech. We must support him in his initiatives. Secondly, we are going to have to discipline ourselves to keep the debate from degenerating. Therefore, we must refrain from making untimely statements. Lastly, if Meech fails, we will be holding a summer caucus in Gaspé, in August, which will be an opportunity for us to take stock." At the time, his words seemed, to me, to be full of common sense. It is worth noting that, in case of failure, he did not foresee a need for the Québec caucus to react until well after the deadline of June 23rd.

After Lucien Bouchard's resignation, Mulroney quickly recovered. He called a meeting with all the provincial

Premiers for one last negotiating session, at the end of
which, on June 9, 1990, the First Ministers came to an
agreement that reflected 90% of the content of our
Committee's report. This was inevitable. We had, after all,
invented nothing. We simply stated the main demands of
those who opposed the Meech Lake Accord. Nevertheless,
that evening, at the signing ceremony that followed the
negotiations, I had a premonition of what lay ahead. I had
been assigned a seat as close as possible to the back,
presumably to avoid my being seen by the television
cameras. In politics, when you fall from grace, you are
physically put aside. So, I was placed as far up in the
bleachers as possible. As I watched the ceremony unfold,
two things happened that clearly foreshadowed what was
to follow. First, Clyde Wells had had an asterisk added to
the document he was agreeing to sign. This asterisk meant
that, in order to come into effect, the approval he had just
given to the final text of the Accord would have to be
submitted to a vote in the legislature of his province.
Then, having signed it, he concluded by saying that we all
had to be "Canadians first and foremost." Such a statement
would sound perfectly routine coming from the mouth of
an American. However, Canada is not a melting-pot. Our
reflexes are different. In Québec, in the highly charged
atmosphere of the time, it was likely his words would be
interpreted as a call for uniformity, if not outright assim-
ilation. It was then I realized that, willfully or otherwise, he
had not understood that what the Meech Lake Accord was
attempting to do was to reconcile different identities. That
evening, therefore, even though all around me everyone
was celebrating, I was very depressed. I was sitting beside
Gérald Beaudoin and Solange Chaput-Rolland, and I said
to them, "It's over".

The very next day, when Prime Minister Mulroney
called me about my reaction, I told him of my concerns. "I
think we are going to have some problems," I said. "I think

it is going to be very hard." He seemed surprised. He was very confident. Right away he answered that there was no problem, that it was going to work out, that Wells had given his word. However, Wells was a peculiar kind of politician, a dogmatist, obstinate and absolutely convinced he was right to the point where he had stopped listening. Moreover, he seemed blinded by the support he was getting from a part of the public that was inundating him with letters pleading with him not to give in.

On June 23, the last day of the three-year deadline for unanimous approval of the Accord by the governments of Canada and all the provinces, I was in Calgary. I had been invited by Radio-Canada to act as a commentator on the federal Liberal Party Leadership Convention. On that day, the very day that Meech failed, Jean Chrétien was elected leader of the federal Liberal Party in Calgary. In Newfoundland, despite the Prime Minister's efforts (he had gone in person to the Newfoundland Legislature to try and persuade recalcitrant M.L.A.s to vote in favour of the Accord), Clyde Wells canceled the vote. In the Legislature of Manitoba, an N.D.P. Aboriginal M.L.A. named Elijah Harper withheld his consent to Meech, thus preventing a unanimous vote that would have enabled his Legislature to give the Accord its final approval. It was a very sad day.

One of the important lessons I learned from that experience concerns the nature of public debate and the incredible fragility of the social peace we take for granted. One of the greatest challenges facing political leaders is learning to distinguish between actions that can have short term and long term consequences in order to make the best possible decisions. Another conclusion I came to was that Meech marked the beginning of a period of affirmation for Aboriginal peoples. In their case, what was happening went well beyond the Meech Lake Accord. For them, a point of no return had been reached. It was then that they collectively decided they had had enough and would no longer accept being told to wait their turn. Coming from a region of Canada where there are few Aboriginal people, I had a lot to learn about their concerns. For me, the defining moment came in Vancouver when Ethel Blondin said to me, "Jean, we can't. We can't wait any longer." That was when I understood that their frustrations had reached such a level that, for them, nothing was possible any more. It was a matter of their survival, and if there is one thing Québecers can understand it is the will to survive.

It was the beginning of a period of affirmation for the Aboriginal peoples of Canada—a movement comparable, in some ways, to that of the francophones in the 1960's. Such an affirmation is not only inevitable, it is desirable. It is a painful process for everyone involved, especially the Aboriginal peoples themselves. It will require them to take full responsibility for their choices and their destiny, but it is a prerequisite to their finding their rightful place in this country. It is an ongoing process, one which will be with us for at least the next twenty years, and it reflects profound changes that are occurring primarily within the Aboriginal communities themselves. As for Elijah Harper, he quickly became a convenient scapegoat for the many people who were only too happy to let him take the rap for the failure of Meech. In Québec, nationalist fervour, whipped up by the PQ and raised to fever pitch by Lucien Bouchard's resignation a few days earlier, exploded on June 24th, Saint Jean Baptiste Day. The sovereignist leadership, with Bouchard at its head, exulted. The strategy of intransigence, the all-or-nothing, take-it-or-leave-it-approach, had borne fruit. As for me, it was the day I turned thirty-two, and a very sad birthday it was.

The Green Plan

The summer that followed was a long one, both in Québec and in the rest of the country. Michou, the children and I spent a few peaceful weeks in the Eastern Townships. In the fall, the House of Commons resumed sitting against a background of stormy public hearings then being held across the country by the Spicer Commission. This Commission was set up to consult Canadians—mainly in the English-speaking provinces—on the best way to move the country forward in the wake of the Meech Lake failure. However, it had turned into a gigantic exercise for the venting of ordinary people's anger and frustration.

I did my best to concentrate on my work as a Member of Parliament. In the spring of 1991, the Prime Minister invited me to rejoin the Cabinet. He entrusted me with the Environment Portfolio and asked me to sit on the Planning and Priorities Committee. It is important to know that in the Mulroney government the Cabinet was so large (it numbered about 40 ministers) it had become a kind of super caucus, which met only every two weeks. The real Cabinet, in the classical sense of the term, was the Planning and Priorities Committee. It met weekly and included about fifteen ministers (which in itself is a quorum to form a Cabinet). To be a member of the "full

Cabinet" was really equivalent to being a member of the "caucus of Ministers." In Canadian politics there is a world of difference between being an M.P. and a Minister, but there are also crucial distinctions between being a Secretary of State and a senior minister. In the Mulroney government, there existed an additional, formal hierarchy between senior ministers, depending on whether they sat on the Planning and Priorities Committee or on the Committee of Operations. The latter was an even more select group of only five or six ministers. It was, in fact, the true decision-making body within the government. By appointing me to the Planning and Priorities Committee, the Prime Minister wanted to show that the Environment was still a priority concern to him.

My interest in the environment went back a long way. During my first campaign, in 1984, I made it a local election issue. Public opinion was becoming seriously concerned about the emergence of major new environmental problems such as global warming. So much so that we planned to put the Environment at the center of our 1988 election platform before Free Trade pushed everything else off the campaign agenda. After the re-election of our government, as Tom McMillan, the Minister of the Environment, had been defeated in his riding in Prince Edward Island, Lucien Bouchard asked for and was given the Environment portfolio. What seemed to interest him at the time was that an important part of the work of the Canadian Environment Minister concerned his relations with his American counterpart. In Canada, the Environment file is largely a Canada-U.S. relations file. We have the longest common border in the world. The Great Lakes, the St. Lawrence, many other rivers whose water and fish we share, air quality and a host of other issues are all matters of concern for both countries. The Minister of the Environment is therefore called upon to be in frequent contact with the U.S. government. More than anything else, that is what, I believe, attracted Lucien Bouchard to the portfolio.

When he was Environment Minister, Bouchard had wanted to launch a "Green Plan". He evidently believed, in order to make your mark in Ottawa, you had to bring forth a big, expensive project. So, he let it be known that his Green Plan was going to cost 10 billion dollars. The initiative prompted a lengthy debate within the government that continued after he left, when Robert-René de Cotret succeeded him. As Environment Minister, de Cotret, who had been President of the Treasury Board, was a wise choice. He was a seasoned technician with an in-depth understanding of how the Federal government worked. Within the government, he was probably the best person to move the Green Plan through the system and ensure that it graduated from the planning stage to actually become government policy. Once the Green Plan, under his stewardship, cleared all the necessary hurdles to become a sustainable development plan, at a cost of $3 billion over six years, the time had come to launch it politically. As it happened, one of the first announcements de Cotret had to make concerned the opening of a $25 million center for research on water quality in the Great Lakes. However, it turned into a full-scale media circus when a Greenpeace activist interrupted the press conference and shouted abuse at de Cotret in full view of the television cameras. It was a communications disaster for the government and the Prime Minister concluded that de Cotret was, perhaps, not the best person to sell the Green Plan to the Canadian Public.

In the Cabinet shuffle that followed, the Prime Minister gave me the responsibility for the Environment. When he did so, he made it very clear that my job was to launch the Green Plan; that it was a little like bringing a child into the world; that I would be responsible for taking care of the "baby" and ensuring its growth; that was my mission. And a significant challenge it was. The department I inherited was a large one. It employed some 15,000 people. I quickly discovered it was made up of a first-rate team of civil servants, scientists, researchers and experts. In short, a group of dedicated, hard-working professionals who believed in the environmental cause. My deputy minister, Len Good, was an exceptionally competent person. I also had a highly capable associate deputy minister in Lorette Goulet. We embarked on our mission with great determination, so much so that we were able to have eighty-seven Cabinet documents approved in the space of eight months—an all-time record. Needless to say, this meant the entire team had to work literally day and night, especially in view of the fact that each one of our initiatives was second-guessed by one or the other of my colleagues at every turn. Indeed, the level of support around the Cabinet table was not strong.

In fact, Lucien Bouchard (who now sat as a Bloc Québecois M.P. in the House of Commons), by his unilateral announcement in Bergen, Norway, in the spring of 1990, had poisoned relations between the department of the Environment and all the other government departments in Ottawa. In hindsight, his actions seemed to indicate that he knew he was leaving and could not have cared less about the consequences. Since then, the shock waves continued to spread throughout the government. Each time I put forth a new proposal someone would say, "But this time, you're not going to do what you did in Bergen. You're not going to act unilaterally!" Actually, it was not me they blamed for the bad blood, but the civil servants in my department who were suspected of having encouraged Bouchard to take the position he had. But they had no say whatsoever in the matter. Every time I came to Cabinet with a new initiative, there was a battle. Still, it was my mission to launch the Green Plan. At the time, it was one of the only plans for sustainable development in the world. Canada was then part of a very small group of countries that had adopted plans for sustainable development.

It is important to understand that for Canada, the environment is a crucial economic issue. Among all of the developed countries, Canada is the one that is the most dependent on its environment to "earn its keep." Our economy is built on forest products (pulp, paper and lumber); on energy (oil, gas, and hydroelectric power); on agriculture (wheat and other crops, dairy products, poultry, beef and pork); on fisheries (which are threatened on both coasts); on the mining sector; and on the management of our water resources and our northern lands. When you think about it, in Canada, the economy *is* the environment. Add to that the fact that, among the industrialized nations, Canada is, with Germany, the country whose economy most relies on exports. That is how vulnerable we are to external markets and the perceptions foreign consumers have of the way we manage our economy and environmental resources. Today, more than ever, the environment is a factor in the decisions consumers make about the products they buy.

At the time, the most striking example of this environmental concern was the pulp and paper industry. Part of my assignment was to update twenty-year-old regulations pertaining to paper mills. The country was just emerging from recession. Moreover, the pulp and paper industry, which is subject to cyclical fluctuations, was at the bottom of a cycle. Despite this, the Canadian Pulp and Paper Association wanted tighter environmental regulations. Why? Because pulp and paper producers suffered from the perception, widespread in foreign countries, that their industry was not adequately regulated. For this reason they were losing out, or risked losing out, on important sales in Europe, particularly in England and Germany. This shows how great an impact environmental management issues can have on our economic future. Another example of this problem is the seal hunt. Canadian seal hunters will tell you their livelihood is part of a way of life that is four hundred years old, older, therefore, than Canada itself and perfectly legitimate. Except that the perception foreign markets have of the seal hunt has caused irreparable damage to the fur industry in Canada. Faced with that, our reaction should be to answer the charges. No matter what the reality is, if the perception among foreign consumers is that we are not managing our resources properly, it is we who suffer; we pay the price. The environment is therefore an economic issue of the highest importance.

The other factor that must be considered is the possibility of a rise in "green protectionism", i.e. the passing of legislation in countries with whom we do business to prevent imports of products that, in their composition or manufacture, do not meet certain environmental standards. If ever a movement of this kind were to become widespread, Canada would be the most vulnerable of countries. We can neither afford to lose ground nor risk being left behind. In any case, the price of failure is simply too high for both our economic prospects and our future generations.

Where Credit is Due

It was not long before I understood why the government was having so much trouble getting its Green Plan message across. No sooner had I arrived in the department, in the spring of 1991, than I had to announce an environmental strategy for the Arctic, in collaboration with the Department of Indian Affairs and Northern Development. For purely practical reasons, it had to be announced without delay. In the Canadian North, the period during which the program could be implemented was so short that unless we launched it almost immediately, we would have to put it off until the following year. Consequently, I was able to get speedy approval from my colleagues for the project.

In the days that followed we traveled to Iqaluit to announce the program jointly with the government of the Territories. This federal government initiative was well received. A significant portion of the funding it included was earmarked for research. At the time, the department did not have a database that enabled us to measure the evolution of the Arctic environment, an environment we suspected was contaminated by the dumping of toxic wastes into the atmosphere by countries of the former Eastern Bloc. We had good reason to suspect the presence

of these pollutants in the food chain of the Arctic, a region
you would have thought was the most pristine on the face
of the Earth. The extremely fragile Arctic ecosystem was
also suffering the effects of global warming, a new
phenomenon that we needed to better understand. We
urgently needed to give ourselves a database.

So we made the trip to Iqaluit and returned to Ottawa
in time to catch the evening newscast. When I turned on
my television I could not believe what I saw. There was the
most important environmental group on northern issues,
roundly denouncing the environmental strategy we had
just made public. I got a frosty reception the next day at
the Cabinet meeting. One of my colleagues put it bluntly:
"So, that was a great announcement, wasn't it? All that, just
to be criticized."

As soon as I got back to my department I ordered an
analysis of what had happened. I could not understand
how so positive an announcement could have come out so
wrong. Finally, I realized that the government had a way of
announcing its initiatives that got everyone's backs up. It
was done without any consultation or involvement of the
environmental groups who, often, had been working on
these issues for years. My conclusion was that the first
thing we should do was to put ourselves in their place.
There were local groups who deserved credit for having
been the first to raise the consciousness of the Canadian
public and government on an environmental issue they
were facing at home. When the day finally came for the
government to move, we neither took the time to recognize their efforts nor gave them the credit they deserved.

Once I understood the problem, I had the department change its ways. In every announcement we made
after that, we took care to recognize and clearly under-
score the work carried out by the citizens or environmental groups concerned. It was the least we could
decently do. Some time later, when we launched a $100

million program for the Fraser River in British-Columbia, we got a better reception. That initiative was followed in rapid succession by dozens of others, and the reactions, all round, began to improve.

HE's here!

In the months that followed, I got to know the fascinating world of environmental politics. One of the first meetings I attended was the Canadian Conference of Environment Ministers, which was held in Halifax in the weeks that followed my swearing in. In preparation for the conference, I chaired a meeting in the board room of the department (there were about fifteen people around the table). I was astonished to find that the first twenty minutes of the meeting were taken up by a single topic: Gordon Perks.

The son of a former editor of the Montreal *Gazette*, Gordon Perks was also a Greenpeace activist in charge of tracking pulp and paper industry issues. His assignment was to heckle the Environment Minister at public events. It was a straightforward public relations exercise managed by Greenpeace. Gordon Perks was also the instigator of the previously mentioned de Cotret communications disaster. Another feather in his cap was his ambushing of David Peterson, then Premier of Ontario, on the day he launched his campaign for re-election in 1990. As Peterson was giving the press conference that marked the official launch to his campaign, Gordon Perks showed up with a tape recorder, chained himself to the table where the

Premier sat answering reporters' questions, turned on his tape recorder and began shouting abuse. That incident marked the beginning of the end for the Peterson campaign. Gordon Perks' specialty was media manipulation.

To get back to my meeting with the officials of my department, the whole discussion centered on knowing whether or not Perks was going to attend the conference in Halifax, which we were preparing. I could not believe my ears. All the senior officials in the department were obsessed by the idea that one person was going to show up at our conference and throw it into disarray. I concluded the meeting by saying, "First, I don't ever again want to spend so much time discussing something like this. There is no way one demonstrator is going to make us waste this much time. If Mr. Perks shows up, I don't want security to be called. I will look after it, and if I need help I will let you know."

We arrived in Halifax a few days later. The first night, I was in my hotel room when I heard a knock at the door. I opened it, and there before me I saw an official from my department, out of breath, sweating visibly and in a state approaching panic. "He's here!" he puffed. As I did not know who he was referring to I asked, "Who?"

"HE's here!"

"Who's here?"

"You don't understand! HE's here!"

"Who are you talking about?"

"GORDON PERKS! He's in the hotel!"

"Oh, him!"

The poor fellow was beside himself predicting havoc, disaster, chaos!

The next day we learned that when the ministers were scheduled to hold their joint press conference to sum up the results of their deliberations, Mr. Perks and an accomplice were planning to hide behind the doors of the meeting room with a trolley-load of petitions and, as soon as

the press conference began, burst into the room with their
petitions, try to take control of the press conference and
embarrass the minister.

Knowing this, just before the press conference was to
begin, I told my Nova Scotia counterpart, John Leef, who
was hosting the conference, "If you don't mind there is
something that needs to be dealt with before we begin.
There is someone here who wants to interrupt our press
conference, so we'll deal with him first and then get on
with it." I asked which door our Mr. Perks was hiding
behind. At the beginning of the press conference I told
the media we would give them a summary of our meeting,
but before we did that, there was someone here who had
something to say and we were going to give that person an
opportunity to speak to them. I got up from my seat,
walked to the door, opened it wide, and there stood Gordon
Perks and his accomplice with their petitions. I asked
Mr. Perks to come in. The media followed. I introduced
Mr. Perks to the media. "Mr. Perks," I said, "has something
he would like to say. We are going to let him do that. Then
we will hold our press conference." Mr. Perks, a little taken
aback, made his statement and asked me to react. Remembering the de Cotret episode, rather than hand him a
spectacle for the cameras, I calmly offered a response that
was as neutral as possible, thanked him, and returned to
my seat. The press conference began without a hitch.
Mr. Perks still got his news item on TV that night, but it
wasn't the disaster feared by officials in my department.
Gordon Perks and I were to cross paths many more times
after that.

On the second anniversary of the Green Plan, I had
to give a speech in Toronto, to a business group, at seven
thirty in the morning. As I entered the hall, I noticed six
television cameras. Right away I could tell something was
up. I was willing to believe my speeches were good, but I
knew they weren't that good—certainly not so good as to

attract six television cameras at seven thirty in the morning in Toronto. The host of the meeting was David Crombie, a former minister in the Mulroney government. As I shook hands around the room I came to a table at which members of Greenpeace were seated, including none other than Gordon Perks. I went to my seat and when the time came for me to give my speech, David Crombie introduced me. As soon as I stood up and headed towards the podium, the Greenpeace group got up from their table, and the television cameras started rolling. Perks and his friends marched up to the podium, lined up behind me and unfurled a banner that read "CHAREST CHARADE/ GREEN PLAN."

So, rather than resist, I simply said, "Ladies and Gentlemen, I would like to introduce to you Gordon Perks. Gordon works for Greenpeace and his job is to follow me everywhere to try as much as possible to interrupt my speeches. Gordon and I have been working together for several years." The audience began to laugh. "But don't worry," I continued. "I'm used to it. You know, it isn't always easy when you are dealing with the environment. Often there are people who have things they want to say to us, and I don't want to keep anyone from expressing themselves. However, I don't intend to get into a contest with Gordon this morning to find out who can speak the loudest. So, ladies and gentlemen, I am pleased to introduce to you Gordon Perks. I am now going to step down from the podium, and when he is finished speaking, I will be happy to continue with my speech. Thank you very much." I then left the podium and Gordon was so surprised he just stared, open-mouthed, at the audience. He did not know what to do, and the people in the room began to boo. He had to leave the stage. From that moment on, everyone in the department stopped worrying about what Gordon was going to do next.

The Earth Summit

As I have shown, the birth of the Green Plan was not an easy one. The "baby" had very nearly been rejected by the government, but it had a powerful sponsor in Prime Minister Mulroney. Among the leaders of the industrialized nations, he was the most proactive on environmental issues. It may be forgotten today, but it was he who engaged the United States government on acid rain. That was no Sunday school picnic. The Reagan government, on ideological grounds, was not overly concerned with environmental problems. It was largely thanks to the perseverance of Mulroney that an agreement on the reduction of emissions causing acid rain was finally concluded with the Americans. He raised the question at his very first official meeting with the U.S. President in Washington, before the 1984 elections, while he was still leader of the Official Opposition. At the "Shamrock Summit" with Reagan in Québec City in 1985, Mulroney, as Prime Minister of Canada, made the issue his personal priority. It was one of the great successes of his political career. The agreement on Air Quality was finally approved by the U.S. Congress in 1990. It had taken six years, and two American administrations, to finally get an outcome that satisfied Canada. And that agreement was preceded by an important initiative aimed at reducing sulfur dioxide emissions in Canada. As Minister of the Environment, I was fortunate to have a Prime Minister who was favourable to the cause I was defending even though he had many additional priorities.

As soon as I arrived in the department, we began preparing the Canadian delegation for the Earth Summit to be held in Rio de Janeiro. The Rio Summit was to be presided over by Maurice Strong, a Canadian who had chaired the first Earth Summit twenty years earlier in Nairobi, Kenya. It should be remembered that this was to be an international conference on the economy and the environment, and, therefore, a major international event. Leaders from most of the nations on the planet would attend. For Canada, the stakes were very high.

Before my arrival at the Ministry of Environment, a senior civil servant named John Bell had the wisdom to include representatives from a broad cross-section of Canadian society in the delegation. In fact, we were the only country to adopt such an approach. This meant that each of our preparatory meetings was attended by representatives from environmental groups, business groups, provincial and municipal governments, non-profit organizations, student associations and youth groups. Realizing that we had an opportunity to assemble a delegation that would be unique, I recruited the director of the Fondation québécoise en environnement, Robert Dubé. He was a childhood friend who, at the time of my first election campaign in 1984, was involved with an environmental group in Sherbrooke. At that time, Robert helped me draft the environmental portion of my election platform. So, I asked him to come to the department to look after our relations with interested parties from outside the government. It was a wise decision. Robert got to work and established a good working relationship with everyone from environmental groups to the Coal Producers Association.

His task was to orchestrate and coordinate the diverse special interests that were going to be represented within our delegation.

From the outset, our approach in preparing the Canadian delegation was different in that it was completely open. The negotiations in Rio were going to focus on two treaties that were to be concluded concerning climate change and biodiversity. A third series of discussions were to take place for the purpose of signing an international agreement on the world's forests. We would have preferred a treaty, but developing countries did not want one. The basic outcomes to be achieved were contained in a document called "Agenda 21."

During our preparations, we made a point of including the provincial governments in all our discussions. This approach was different and it worked. Provincial government representatives had free access to the federal officials involved in the process, as did the environmental groups and all the other interested parties. In this way we were able to create a process that was completely open, and the team we assembled reflected that. If, for example, a group concerned with energy issues wanted to make a proposal to modify the Canadian position, it could by making a direct submission to the official mandated by the government to make changes to Canada's position. This was new for many people. It had never been done before and it enabled us to share in a unique experience.

The Canadian delegation in Rio met every morning around a large table. Sometimes there were one hundred and fifty people in the room. As head of the delegation, I chaired these meetings. It was important to me that people know they had been heard without having to go through twenty different channels and having their comments filtered or modified before they reached the ears of the person ultimately in charge. During the morning meetings, the different officials reported on the state of the negotiations. The people seated around the table then reacted and made recommendations, but the other people in the room were also invited to participate. If a member of an environmental group wanted to suggest that Canada should insist on a point, he or she could raise a hand and argue their position. We would seek a consensus, which we would then go out and defend. It was an unforgettable experience and such a resounding success that, afterwards, provincial governments across Canada adopted the provisions of both treaties without hesitation, even though the treaty on biodiversity touched on areas of provincial jurisdiction. This harmonization occurred without opposition because the provincial governments were a part of the process from the very beginning. The Canadian government was not behaving paternalistically and saying, "We signed this. We are responsible for signing international agreements, and here is what we decided." The signed document reflected a true consensus to which the provinces directly contributed. I find this experience especially memorable because it holds important lessons for the future of federalism.

Is There a Translator in the Room?

The high point of the Rio Summit came at the very beginning when the G7 countries met. The G77 countries, headed by Malaysia and India, were meeting simultaneously. Some time before, the G7 Environment Ministers held a preparatory meeting in Bonn. That meeting almost failed to take place because each of our External Affairs departments were opposed to the idea of the Environment Ministers meeting amongst themselves. The experience taught me a great deal about the workings of international institutions. For instance, one of the great strengths of the G7 is that it has no bureaucracy. From its inception, it was decided that heads of government would meet without their officials. This policy avoided the pitfalls of the UN model, which was rife with bureaucratic red tape. However, one of the consequences of that decision was that governments had to agree not to create all kinds of parallel bodies, which is why only the G7 Finance Ministers met regularly. So, when the G7 Environment Ministers wanted to convene to discuss the positions to be adopted at the Earth Summit, our respective Foreign Affairs departments balked. In the end, the preparatory meeting went ahead anyway.

We met again as soon as we arrived in Rio. The outcome of this second meeting was that the Bush administration, then in the midst of an election campaign, was ideologically opposed to both the treaty on climate change and the one on biodiversity. Consequently, the U.S. was going to refuse to sign either one. With Arthur Campeau, Canada's Ambassador to the Earth Summit in Rio, I telephoned Prime Minister Mulroney, then in Canada. I informed him that if we wanted to break the logjam, a G7 country was going to have to announce, now, that it would sign both treaties. We were the only country that seemed inclined to take this first step. If we did not, it was probable that the conference was going to end in failure because other countries would take refuge behind the U.S. refusal and not sign the treaties. It was not an easy decision for Mulroney. President Bush was running for re-election. Such an action by Canada risked embarrassing an ally and Mulroney did not wish to interfere with the internal affairs of the United States. At the same time, and this is where he showed the Irish side of his temperament, he wanted to make the right decision for Canada. On our recommendation, he authorized us to announce that Canada would sign both treaties. As expected, the other G7 countries all followed suit, except the Americans who resisted to the end.

I first met Al Gore in Rio. He was then a U.S. Senator with a strong interest in environmental issues. Pierre-Marc Johnson, the brother of Daniel Johnson and a former PQ Premier of Québec, was also at the conference. Johnson's expertise in the environmental field was already internationally recognized, and he gave us some valuable advice. All this enabled Canada to make its mark at the Conference, and the credit for that belongs to Brian Mulroney (who, incidentally, once he arrived in Rio, chaired two of the morning meetings of the Canadian delegation).

If I was up early every morning, I was also up late every night. As soon as I returned to the hotel at the end of the day, we had a series of meetings with officials from our department and the Canadian International Development Agency (CIDA) to prepare our positions for the next day. Among the important—and controversial—issues for Canada was our commitment to devote 0.7% of Canada's Gross National Product to foreign aid. As we were in a period of budget restraint, it proved extremely difficult to obtain a consensus on that point within our government. The other controversial issue was forestry. Here we saw an interesting development that clearly illustrated the economic-environmental link I mentioned earlier. The forestry industry associations, like pulp, paper and lumber producers, wanted a treaty on the world's forests because, in the absence of internationally recognized standards, they had no way of defending themselves against accusations that they were harming the environment. Forestry producers were saying to us, "We prefer a treaty, with rules we know we can surpass, to the no-win situation we now have." That being said, developing countries, led by Malaysia and India, vehemently opposed any international regulation of the forest industry and accused developed countries of wanting to practice a form of economic colonialism.

The dean of the G7 Environment Ministers was Klaus Topfer, the highly respected German Environment Minister who was a skilled negotiator. Topfer had five years experience with the Environment Portfolio in the government of Helmut Kohl. In Rio, he often spoke for the G7 when we met with the G77. Topfer had an unusual habit: whenever the subject of forests came up, he would preface his remarks by saying, in his very pronounced German accent, "In forestry, we need clear-cut solutions." Finally, during a bilateral meeting, I said to the minister, "Klaus, do me a favour. Stop saying *In forestry we need clear-cut solutions*. In my country, it just won't fly." I then explained to him the other meaning of the expression "clear-cut"…

During another negotiating session on forests, the discussions of the Contact Group[3] had reached an impasse. Therefore, it was decided to broaden the discussion to involve a number of developing and developed countries, including Canada. The meeting was held late in the evening, around 10 p.m. I arrived in the meeting room with our forestry negotiator. We all sat down around a large table. The meeting, chaired by Klaus Topfer, included environment ministers from several French-speaking African countries. Topfer began explaining, in his laboured English, the main sticking points that had to be resolved in order to break the impasse. Suddenly, the Environment Minister of an African country stood up and demanded simultaneous translation into French. The thirty-odd people around the table exchanged long looks. There was no interpreter in the room and we all knew that we were going to be up negotiating through a good part of the night. Topfer, knowing he could not force his colleague to negotiate, was in a bind because there was no possibility of finding a translator at that time of night. In the end, I raised my hand and offered to act as interpreter. Topfer was only too glad to accept.

The African minister, however, was not at all pleased with my offer, but could not refuse. So, I sat down next to him and, as Topfer spoke, I translated. I knew his purpose for making the request had not really been to obtain an interpreter as much as to scupper the negotiations. As it happened, his strategy had just run aground. I kept translating for about twenty minutes, at which point my African colleague turned to me in exasperation and hissed, "ENOUGH!" The negotiations that night dragged on until three o'clock in the morning.

---

[3] Contact Group: select group of negotiators representing the G7 and G77 countries.

Olivia!

We worked literally day and night—from six a.m. to the wee hours of the morning. Over the two weeks of the conference, we had only one day, Sunday, off. Because the city of Rio has a reputation for being dangerous, the Brazilian Army practically emptied the city of its youth, its homeless, and, in short, anyone else who, in the eyes of the Brazilian government, might interfere with the Summit being held in a conference center just outside the city. On our one and only Sunday off, the Brazilian government organized a press conference to highlight the link between sports and the environment. It was a promotional event that included the awarding of a medal and an honourable mention to the Canadian government. This media event was presided by Olivia Newton-John and John Denver, who were ambassadors to the Rio summit, and the Conference chairman, Canadian Maurice Strong.

For my part, I did not wish to attend the press conference. I considered it to be little more than a photo-op that was going to deprive me of my day off with Michou. "Send someone else," I said to my staff. "I really don't want to be part of a media event today." That was when we learned that Pele, the famous Brazilian soccer player, was expected to attend. You, kind reader, may have forgotten my passion for that sport. My deputy ministers, however, remembered that I played soccer as a youngster and jumped at the opportunity to inform me of Pele's presence at the press conference. I relented.

Michou and I arrived at the press conference that afternoon. It should be noted that thousands of journalists were covering the Rio summit, so the room was packed. We managed to squeeze our way through the compact crowd that bristled with microphones and television cameras. The press conference began. Suddenly, who do we see arriving in the room but Bianca Jagger. All the cameras swivelled in her direction while, at the front, the press conference carried on, practically inaudible in the general pandemonium. After a while the cameras turned around and focused once again on the people giving the press conference. Then, who walks into the room but Shirley Maclaine. At that moment the Brazilian Environment Minister had just taken the floor. Seeing all the cameras turned towards Shirley Maclaine and realizing he had no hope of competing with her for the attention of the media, he invited her to join him at the front, which she promptly did. As soon as she sat down, the Brazilian handed her the microphone and she launched into a withering denunciation of the Bush Administration. Everyone was listening, a little ill at ease, when all of a sudden the Beach Boys entered the room. The press conference was turning into a kind of 1960s-style "happening." Michou and I could only look at each other and say, "I don't believe this!" At that point, Jerry Brown, the eccentric ex-governor of California who was then running for U.S. President, arrived. To my great disappointment, the only person who didn't show up was Pele!

When the press conference ended, everyone was supposed to gather for a march along the beach. But first, members of the Canadian delegation were waiting to join us. They had a gigantic Canadian flag bearing thousands

of signatures of Canadian citizens that had been collected
before our departure from Canada through Canadian Tire
stores across the country. I was to mount a podium and say
a few words on behalf of Canada. We were surrounded by
a crush of people amid total confusion. When I climbed
onto the stage, it was so crowded I could feel the floor
boards sag beneath me. People in the crowd were yelling,
"Shirley Maclaine! Shirley Maclaine!" I yelled back, "I'm
not Shirley Maclaine!" The microphone would not work.
Finally, I got off the stage and we started our march to the
beach, surrounded by other Canadians, with the huge
Canadian flag up at the front. Suddenly, three people
rushed past us carrying the French environmentalist Jacques
Cousteau on their shoulders. A Radio-Canada reporter,
accompanied by his cameraman, stopped me and asked
for a brief interview. I said a few words as the crowd began
to gather round us.

We started walking again when someone approached
Michou, whose blond hair was then shoulder length, and
asked for her autograph. Soon, someone else did the
same. At that, several television cameras from Brazilian,
Spanish and Argentinian networks stopped us and someone began shouting "Olivia! Olivia!" obviously mistaking
Michou for Olivia Newton-John. Around us people jostled
each other. Michou and I got separated. Finally, the RCMP
officers who accompanied us managed to lead us away.
Pointing to a hotel on the other side of the road they
yelled, "At the count of three, start running!" We took off
as fast as our legs would carry us and ducked into the
hotel… It was a crazy adventure—one neither Michou nor
I will soon forget.

Great Whale

The Great Whale Hydroelectric Project, on the Great Whale River in northern Québec, was a project dear to Québec Premier Robert Bourassa. The environmental assessment of the Great Whale project was an extremely complex issue because it involved an area covered by the James Bay and Northern Québec Agreement (JBNQA)— an agreement between the Crees, the Inuit, the governments of Québec and Canada, Hydro-Québec, the Société de développement de la baie James, and the Société d'énergie de la baie James. This agreement, the first of its kind in Canada, is considered a treaty and recognized as such under the Canadian Constitution. However, very few people at that time had a sufficient understanding of its provisions to fully appreciate all of its implications.

For a project the size of Great Whale, the JBNQA provided for four separate environmental assessments. However, the Bourassa government was stubbornly refusing to compromise with opponents of the project, i.e. environmental groups and the Aboriginal peoples—Cree and Inuit—inhabiting the territory in question. As Minister of the Environment for the Canadian government, I had no choice in the matter because the Supreme Court of Canada had recently ruled that the federal government was obliged to respect its own environmental assessment legislation. So, I had to proceed with the environmental assessment of the Great Whale project, parts of which impacted on fields of federal jurisdiction.

After the Cabinet meeting that produced the decision to proceed with the environmental assessment of the Great Whale Project, the Prime Minister asked me to go to Québec City to explain our position to Premier Robert Bourassa. It happened that on that very day an article about Great Whale appeared in *Time* Magazine. By going to Québec City, one of the things I wanted to do was verify whether or not the Bourassa government was aware of what was being said in the United States concerning Québec's environmental record. My meeting with Premier Bourassa was very cordial. However, at the end of my conversation with him, I was not reassured. He did not give me the impression that his government was conscious of the negative impact the Great Whale Project was having on its, and Québec's, reputation abroad. The Crees of Northern Québec were then waging a highly effective campaign against the project in the United States. Part of their campaign consisted of asking American public institutions not to buy Hydro-Québec bonds. This further illustrates the economic importance of environmental issues. We should not underestimate the economic consequences of those kinds of decisions on the part of our neighbours. They can be very serious.

The problem we had in Québec was that our politicians, editorialists, business people and union leaders, all had the same reflex, which was to lash out. People were indignant about the Cree campaign, saying, "We're right, they're wrong, and they have no business washing our dirty laundry in our neighbour's yard and tarnishing Québec's reputation abroad." It was an understandably human reaction. But you had to ask yourself whether it really served Québec's long-term interests. It was injurious to our interests to dismiss these objections rather than respond to them. The worst reflex is to recoil, to turn inward. The most positive thing we could do for ourselves was to undertake an open and credible environmental assessment of the Great Whale Project. Unfortunately, and despite the recent Supreme Court Rulings that clearly told us that our own regulations obliged us to undertake an assessment, the Québec government saw our position as federal government interference in the internal affairs of the province. Further complicating the situation was the fact that a federal bill on environmental assessment was in preparation but not ready to be tabled. Among the Québec journalists covering environmental issues, only one, Louis-Gilles Francoeur of *Le Devoir*, managed to write articles that correctly explained the reality of the process.

Therefore, I went to Montreal to announce the federal government's decision to proceed with the environmental assessment of the Great Whale project. With me was Michel Dorais, the senior civil servant responsible for the Federal Environmental Assessment and Review Office (FEARO). This was after Meech, after Oka and after the Bélanger-Campeau Commission. In such an atmosphere, the announcement immediately raised a furor in Québec. The reaction of the business community in particular was extremely negative.

Then began the long process of negotiations in search of an agreement. At the table sat the Crees, the Inuit, the Government of Québec and the Government of Canada. Keeping a watchful eye on the proceedings were environmental groups and representatives from a business community that was still reeling from the effects of a recession. The latter was demanding some kind of economic activity, a power project, anything to jump-start Québec's ailing economy. What happened next allowed me to draw the conclusion that problems, which at first glance look insoluble, can be resolved, providing you find the right people, listen a great deal, show patience, and deal candidly with everyone involved. It is possible to arrive at solutions and resolve differences, with Aboriginal peoples as with others, including those who, at first, seem the most radical. It was our good fortune that someone thought to ask Armand Couture, who at the time was working for Hydro-Québec, to negotiate the agreement.

Armand Couture is not a well-known figure in Québec. He negotiated the JBNQA for the Société d'énergie de la baie James and knew the players as well as the various structures and mechanisms created by the Agreement. He also knew the stakes. It is largely thanks to him that an agreement was finally reached to combine the four environmental assessment processes provided for by the JBNQA into a single one. This combined process managed to meet everyone's criteria and concerns.

I remember signing that agreement at two o'clock in the morning in an office in the Hydro-Québec Building in Montreal. Everyone finally shook hands. The problem was solved. What a relief that was. Personally, it had certainly not been pleasant to be pilloried in the media on a daily basis. But what struck me most was the lengths to which the Government of Québec seemed to go to ignore even its own long-term interests. For it was not in its interest, or in the interest of Québecers, to behave as it did, turning a deaf ear to objections and concerns that eventually reverberated south of the border. Neither did it serve our interests, as Québecers or as Canadians, for the government to simply steamroll its opponents. It was a serious mistake. I often say you should never underestimate the capacity of governments to make mistakes. In fact, the bigger they are, the bigger their mistakes are likely to be. If there is one thing that baffles me, it is when I hear someone say, "After all, they are the government, so they must know what they are doing." You should never presume that governments know what they are doing.

Lucien Was Hiding

As Minister of the Environment, I had to table the Environmental Assessment Bill, a task that proved to be most difficult. At that time, Canada had a set of environmental regulations that had been given a very strict interpretation by the Supreme Court. The government was obliged to apply them to any project that touched on a field of federal jurisdiction. When it comes to the environment, federal jurisdiction covers a broad area that includes, among other things, protection of the seas, the Arctic, the fisheries, sea mammals, migratory birds, and international relations regarding the environment. To manage all those issues, Canada had not yet given itself a coherent set of rules. It was in our interest to do so for the reasons I have already stated. In the meantime, in the absence of the appropriate legislation, any major project was open to challenge on almost any grounds.

We got to work with all the provincial governments that made up the Canadian Council of Environment Ministers except Québec, which, in the wake of the Meech failure, was boycotting the meetings. Pierre Paradis, then Québec's Environment Minister, was highly regarded by his colleagues but was not present at these discussions. Misunderstandings are frequent in situations of that kind. While the Environment Ministers from the other provinces did not find every aspect of our bill to their liking, they agreed to a number of compromises. Pierre, however, was under the impression that we were preparing a bill that was in fact different from the drafts he was seeing. As it happened, the provincial government whose position was closest to that of Québec was Alberta, in the person of then Environment Minister Ralph Klein. It was during those meetings that Ralph and I grew to know each other.

The time finally came to table the bill, which, ironically, had been initiated by Lucien Bouchard when he was the Federal Minister of the Environment. When he was in that position, it has to be said that he took a very hard line with the Government of Québec. If truth be told, all those then involved will tell you there was never a more centralist federal minister of the environment than Lucien Bouchard. To prove it, you need only read over some of his statements. For instance: "My department will have as its policy to establish national standards and to ask that they be respected," he declared on June 26, 1989[4], i.e. less than a year before his resignation in May 1990. And, "We will publish our own national standards according to the Canadian legislation on environmental protection in areas of federal jurisdiction and we will then allow the provinces to establish their own regulations, but these will have to conform with national standards. We want uniformity across the country."[5] Food for thought...

---

[4] See *Comités*, p. 13-12, 26 June 1989.

[5] See also his speech of November 3, 1989, in which he declared: "It is hard to see how a federal constitution could confer to one or the other jurisdiction an area that by definition covers so many topics... Environmental protection, more than any other field, requires close and productive collaboration between the government of Canada and those of the provinces... Cooperation is imperative in every case, as is the harmonization of policies, laws and regulations, based when necessary on national standards... The Federal government will continue to show vigilance in the area of international relations, fisheries, criminal law, interprovincial pollution, navigation and northern regions. It will, when necessary, base its interventions on the notion of peace, order and good government, invoking the national interest, as the Supreme Court of Canada has already authorized it to do in certain cases."

In preparing the bill we consulted with provincial governments, the business community, environmental groups and other interested parties. Their participation was important to us. It was not always easy because the special interests each represented were often very different, but we finally succeeded in drafting legislation and having it approved by the Cabinet.

I was attending the Conference of Environment Ministers in British Columbia when, quite suddenly, I heard that objections to the bill were being voiced by members of our Québec caucus. I hurried back from Vancouver to meet with the caucus, including some Senators who expressed reservations. During that meeting, I was finally able to get across the point that the environment is not in itself an area of jurisdiction—it is an associated responsibility, like employment or the economy, for which the federal government can no more be held solely responsible than can any one provincial government. The economy, employment, etc. are corollaries of the responsibilities properly held by each level of government. Thus, there is an economic dimension to things like transportation or communications. The same goes for the environment.

Strictly from the standpoint of Québec's interests, one of the advantages of the federal system is precisely that it shares environmental responsibility between the two levels of government. It is what gives Québecers a say, and a certain amount of influence, in the decisions made by neighbouring provinces that can affect them. Influence is something we do not have when it comes to decisions made in certain American states. We can inform them of our position, but we have no direct means of shaping the decisions they make that affect us. This lack of influence would be even more pronounced in the case of an independent Québec—one having to independently defend its interests against the American giant. However, as incredible as it may seem, some people, even some outside the sovereignist camp, claimed the opposite was true. The Allaire Report, for example, would have made the environment an exclusive, provincial jurisdiction. This position is patently absurd and can only be explained by the incredible degree to which the constitutional debate had degenerated since the failure of Meech.

I finally tabled the bill in Parliament. I then testified before a Senate Committee. We had to fight to get it adopted and, in the end, we did—but it wasn't easy. When the bill was voted on in the House of Commons, the Bloc Québecois was against it. But one member of Parliament was conspicuously absent that day. While the House was adopting the Canadian Environmental Protection Act he had initiated and in which he had so strongly believed, Mr. Bouchard was in the building, hiding in his office.

A Leader

To understand what happened next, it helps to remember the circumstances. After Meech failed, nearly everything we did as a government came down to trying to "put the toothpaste back in the tube." The hurricane had passed but it had left a lot of damage in its wake that we were doing our often clumsy best to repair... Which brings us back to the importance of understanding the nature of the constitutional changes you are attempting to propose. Just as changes to the foundations of a house require meticulous planning, so do changes to the constitutional foundations of our country. But we had no regrets about the Meech Lake Accord. At the time we had every reason to believe it could be done. All the signals had been positive. What we could not have foreseen was the aftermath.

In the 1991 Cabinet shuffle, the Prime Minister gave Joe Clark the Intergovernmental Affairs portfolio—a significant gesture on Mulroney's part. He was giving his former rival, the man who had once promoted a vision of the country based on the notion of a "community of communities," the responsibility for finding a way to bring the Government of Québec back to the constitutional negotiating table. He then formed a Cabinet Committee on Canadian Unity chaired by Joe Clark. On this Committee sat ministers from across the country: Don Mazankowski, Barbara MacDougall, Kim Campbell, Harvey Andre, and Québecers Marcel Masse, Benoît Bouchard, Gilles Loiselle and myself—all senior ministers. And, on an exceptional basis, the Prime Minister himself was directly involved in the work of the Committee. He did not usually sit on Cabinet committees except the most important ones like the Priorities and Planning Committee. A Prime Minister cannot do everything and should in fact avoid interfering with the proceedings of Cabinet Committees. The Prime Minister must let government ministers do their work. But when it came to National Unity the issue was so vitally important that Prime Minister Mulroney decided to chair the meetings himself whenever he could.

The Committee decided to travel across the country and, naturally, our every move attracted intense media scrutiny. Even though the meetings were confidential, a horde of journalists was hot on our heels everywhere we went. In the end, these deliberations allowed the government to produce a document on Unity. A parliamentary committee, the Dobbie-Edwards Committee, was then set up to carry the ball. The problem was that the going got rougher at every step. You sensed that you were not at the beginning of a new process, but rather floundering in the wake of a previous failure. There was less and less open-mindedness and flexibility as time went on. People's positions on all kinds of issues were becoming more and more entrenched. It was getting harder and harder to get them to budge.

Meanwhile, in Québec, Robert Bourassa was attempting to manage an extremely fragile political situation. The hearings of the Bélanger-Campeau Commission were saturating the media. Sovereignists were having a field day making the most out of Québecers' feelings of rejection. The rhetoric was becoming so intransigent, so all-or-nothing, that any sign of openness or compromise on the part of the Bourassa government was vehemently condemned. In the rest of the country the Reform party played right into the Sovereignists' hands. Everything came to a head around the Referendum on the Charlottetown Constitutional Accord, which was another painful setback for the Mulroney government and another victory for the forces seeking to polarize and divide Canadians. The whole Meech and post-Meech period was one of the most difficult in our country's recent history and should give pause to those who dream of negotiating secession in "peace and serenity." We were in the midst of a deep political crisis that eclipsed even the most pressing economic issues. For the government of Canada, as for the government of Québec, all other matters became secondary.

In the course of these events, the question of Brian Mulroney's future did not arise. In view of our disastrous standing in the polls, he impressed us with his perseverance. They say everything in politics is a matter of timing and, as it happened, one of the decisions we made, one we could not have made at a worse time, was to abolish the federal manufacturers sales tax. It was a hidden tax, one that did not appear separately in the price paid by the consumer. The tax with which we decided to replace it, the infamous GST, was going to show up on every bill and invoice.

The decision to introduce the GST was courageous and well illustrates Mulroney's character. He was very lucid in the way he presented it to us, telling both his Cabinet and his caucus that, politically, it was going to cost us dearly and that it would be very difficult to get people to accept it. He repeated those warnings on several occasions. Each time, he would conclude his remarks by saying, "We are doing it because it is the right decision for the country. Don't expect recognition for it. It is a painful change, but it is necessary." I recognized his Irish temperament in those words. He had mulled over the issue in his head, taken it to heart, and was prepared to face the consequences.

Mulroney's performance was phenomenal during those months. He knew how to persuade his caucus. Every week he had to face a caucus of elected members who wanted to be re-elected but were subjected to the complaints of discontented voters and were daily told, again and again, that they were going to get trounced. Yet he was able to inspire them, to motivate them, and make them believe. To me, that was an example of true leadership. A leader must, even in the worst situations, be able to look further than the people around him. The first test of leadership is to believe when those around us resist or even refuse to believe. Leadership is all about being able to overcome the reservations, second-guessing, doubts and fears of others. That being said, we could feel that our leader considered a good part of his political goals accomplished. The Meech Lake failure weighed heavily on his heart, but he knew he had done all he could and did not fear being judged on his record. He told us, "I have done what I could. It did not work out, but history will be the judge."

A Phoney War

Under those circumstances I began thinking about my own future. I came to the conclusion that if Mr. Mulroney were to leave—as seemed increasingly likely—I would be a candidate in the race to succeed him, even though I did not know in advance who my rivals would be. During the Christmas season of 1992, I began making a few phone calls to colleagues to find out if they thought it would be a good idea for me to run as a candidate in the event that Prime Minister Mulroney were to step down. This was a delicate matter because, for the time being, he was still there. He was not going to say anything as long as his mind was not made up. If I took the liberty of raising the matter with colleagues, it was because Kim Campbell was already working the field. We were hearing about fund raising events and recruiting drives, and the people around me who wanted to see me in the running for the leadership of the Conservative Party urged me to start testing the waters. Out of respect for Prime Minister Mulroney I wanted to be as discreet as possible, but it was nonetheless difficult.

All this activity soon prompted a reaction. At our first Cabinet meeting in January, Mulroney was livid. He ordered those who had the temerity to ask themselves "the question" to cease and desist and get on with their work. I immediately felt his comments were aimed at me and put an end to my activities. But Kim Campbell did nothing of the kind. We could sense it but were being told that this was not the case. Then the whole question arose as to whether or not Mulroney favoured her as a candidate. I do not believe he did. But it is true he wanted to see a whole new generation of leadership candidates—it was no secret. He said so repeatedly. When the race finally began, he repeated that his ardent wish was to see Bernard Valcourt, Jean Charest, Barbara MacDougall and Perrin Beatty enter the race. He wanted a hotly contested leadership race with several high calibre candidates. I did not blame him. In that sense, he encouraged everyone to run.

By the spring of 1993 we were entering the fifth year of a mandate that was to end in November. We were approaching the moment of truth. Mulroney announced he was leaving. That morning, the people around me held a meeting. It was very quickly learned that the main party backers who were close to Mulroney were not only working for Kim Campbell but had begun fund-raising even before the Prime Minister had announced his departure. This had an immediate impact on the leadership race. The way the rank and file interpreted it was that Mr. Mulroney was backing Kim Campbell for the leadership of the Party. It is also worth remembering that all this was happening in the wake of the January Cabinet shuffle that had been relatively limited in scope but had seen the elevation of Kim Campbell to the Ministry of National Defense. That move was interpreted by many as a personal gesture of support on the part of the Prime Minister.

The events of that first morning were decisive. From that moment on, a kind of signal went out through the Party: Kim Campbell was the outgoing Prime Minister's favoured candidate. Whether or not this was true is not important. What mattered was the interpretation given to it. This was the atmosphere in which I had to decide if I was going to run. The decision was painful for me. First of all, if I decided to go for it, it would not be for the sake of appearances. Given the experience I had, I was not going to risk my reputation and financial future just to guarantee myself a place at the Cabinet table or to position myself for the next time. It simply wasn't worth it. On the one hand I did not need to aspire to a Cabinet post, and on the other, I was young enough to be able to start anew in another occupational field.

To get back to the personal side of things, there are few events in political life that put you so completely in the media spotlight as a leadership race. First, as in a contest for the party nomination in a riding, you are left to your own devices. You have to defend your positions without the help of the Party apparatus and all that it entails. You alone have to defend the ideas you put forward. In addition, you are under constant media scrutiny. The campaign lasts three months. You have a microphone thrust under your nose every time you open your mouth. You are always expected to have something to say about everything that happens and every issue that arises. In that sense it is a real test, and it is a good test. A hotly contested leadership race tests candidates and their ideas and is good for a political party.

More than assessing my chances of winning, my greatest preoccupation was determining if I was going to be able to assemble the financial backing necessary to get me there. The history of leadership races teaches us that losers, whether they come second, third or fourth, always end up with debts. Even winners go into debt. The history of political parties is littered with horror stories of people who ran for the leadership of their party and ended up saddled with personal debts for years afterward. I was thirty-four, the father of three children, and I had absolutely no wish to go into debt for the rest of my days. But I was lucky in that I entrusted my brother Robert with managing my campaign expenses. In a leadership campaign the only thing more difficult than raising money is managing it once you have it because anyone around you can claim to spend money on your behalf.

Robert and I lived on the same street in Hull. We both bought houses in a new subdivision. We were neighbours living a few hundred feet away from each other and I remember well what I said to him: "You are going to supervise my campaign spending. I want, absolutely, to avoid going into debt. I especially don't want to be forced to sell my house. In any case, I am warning you right now: If I lose my house, we're moving into yours!" There's nothing like a little incentive to motivate a fellow...

What followed was unbelievable. All the high calibre candidates aspiring to succeed Brian Mulroney, like Barbara MacDougall, Perrin Beatty, Mike Wilson, Don Mazankowski, Benoît Bouchard and Bernard Valcourt, bowed out of the race one after the other under the pretext that Kim Campbell had already won and it would be impossible to beat her. As for me, the more other people decided not to run, the more determined I became. I told myself, "This is not right. This is not the way it's going to be." I had witnessed enough leadership contests to know how volatile and unpredictable they can be, and what a test they truly are.

In the end, out of respect for Mulroney, I went to see him. Some thought I received assurances from him or he persuaded me to throw my hat in the ring. He did strongly encourage me to do so and repeated that he hoped several other candidates would come forward. In that respect, he said the same things to me privately as he said publicly. But my mind wasn't made up. Meanwhile, the situation was evolving. Kim Campbell's organization began to look more and more like a steamroller. It seemed inevitable that she would win, almost to the point where it seemed futile to run against her.

A Call from Rwanda

The people around me were divided on the issue of whether I should run. In a situation like that you are really on your own. There were people close to me and members of my immediate family who advised me not to run, period. The majority of my friends were opposed to the idea. They had analyzed the situation and had come to the conclusion that it was a lost cause. It was up to me to weigh all this advice. Taking everything into account, I refused to close the door because I really felt like running.

I set myself a deadline, March 16th, which was the date of the annual fund raising dinner organized by my Sherbrooke riding association. I decided I would announce my decision, either way, at that event. As a result, the dinner grew to the point where fifteen hundred people bought tickets. My close collaborators were impatiently awaiting my decision. The day finally came when I had to go to Sherbrooke to put an end to the suspense. Michou and I left home to drive Amélie, then ten years old, to school. Along the way we listened to the Radio-Canada news. They mentioned I was to announce my decision that night. Amélie, quite spontaneously, turned towards me and asked: "Well, are you going to run or not?"

"Well, I don't know yet," I said, "what do you think?"

"Do you think you would make a good Prime Minister?"

"Yes."

"Well then, go ahead!"

I was surprised. I chuckled to myself: "Well, that's simple. I wonder why I didn't think of that." We dropped Amélie off at school and headed for Sherbrooke. Then all hell broke loose. My cellular phone wouldn't stop ringing. With bad memories of the Charlottetown Referendum still fresh in our minds (cellular telephone conversations had been tapped and the transcripts leaked to the media), I kept stopping to return the calls from public telephones along the way. I can see myself now, in the McDonald's at the Rigaud exit, standing between two pay-phones holding one receiver over each ear. A woman recognized me, asked to shake my hand, hurried off to her car to get her daughter and returned with her camera. In the meantime I was carrying on simultaneous conversations with people I wanted to consult before arriving in Sherbrooke.

When we arrived, I assembled my staff and we had a debate. It was two o'clock in the afternoon. The fund-raiser was due to begin at six. I was scheduled to speak at seven. And my mind still wasn't made up. The people around me were clearly divided: the majority were against, some were neutral, and a minority encouraged me to enter the race.

Michou, Jean-Bernard Bélisle, Albert Painchaud, George Maclaren, and my brother Robert were with me in the room. Jodi White was on the phone from British-Columbia. Then I got a call from Denis Beaudoin, who had recruited me into the Party ten years before and had given me excellent advice ever since. He was calling from Rwanda where he held a foreign affairs posting. He pleaded eloquently in favour of my entering the race saying it would be a unique opportunity for me to free myself from Party constraints and speak about the things that really mattered. He argued that I could run a grass-roots campaign to restore hope to a population demoralized by the recession. He reminded me that the reforms we had imposed on the country demanded a great deal from Canadians; people needed hope; they needed a government and a Prime Minister capable of setting their sights on the next century; someone to show how it was still possible to build together. He added only someone who was young could really be the bearer of those hopes and dreams.

Once I hung up, Michou and I remained alone in my office. I still wasn't convinced. After a few minutes the telephone rang and I was told it was Denis Beaudoin calling back. We all re-assembled in my office and Beaudoin, once again, vigorously pleaded his case. Michou sat watching me intently from the other side of the desk. She was visibly moved. Beaudoin said, "Jean, you can't not run. The future of the country is at stake; you are made for this. Believe me, you won't have to spend that much money. You don't have to run an expensive campaign. Just rent a bus and go on the road, you'll see."

I listened closely to what he had to say and then, finally, I said, "I'll do it." Everyone broke into applause. Now we had to write my speech. Already four o'clock in the afternoon, it was a nightmare. I had friends writing notes for me in the next room, knowing full well that I was not going to use them. I am not very good at reading speeches unless I write the text myself. Reading other people's words doesn't work for me. That night in Sherbrooke, I delivered my speech live on CBC Newsworld (RDI did not yet exist). The people in the audience were happy. It was the official start of my campaign. Overall, it was a successful launch and the fund-raiser provided an initial contribution to my leadership campaign.

That night around midnight, Michou and I left Sherbrooke for the long drive home. The weather was awful—

very cold with a freezing rain. The wind was howling as I
have rarely heard it howl before or since. We arrived home
around three o'clock in the morning. I had to get up early
the next day to appear on *Canada-AM* on CTV, at seven. I
went to bed and I remember the feeling I had as I drifted
off to sleep: I said to myself, "What have I done? I am
going to lose everything. This can't be. I'm going to lose
my house." It's the feeling you get when you have just
taken the plunge into the unknown. It is the worst time.
You don't know how you are going to land. You are in
utter darkness between earth and sky. We all experience
such moments at some time or other in our lives. Then, all
you have is your faith and your confidence in the future.
You say to yourself, "I don't know how, but I am going to
get through this." You almost wish you could simply
announce the next day that you were just kidding...

Learning to Expect
the Unexpected

Our campaign got under way very quickly. We put together a campaign team; it was one of the most rewarding experiences of our lives. Michou has fond memories of it to this day. We got on a bus and went on the road as Denis Beaudoin had recommended. We started off with nothing. In the first poll that came out after I entered the race we were at 5% while Kim Campbell was at 35%. We were starting with just crumbs of support. Now when people talk to me about polls and tell me I should be happy because I am at such and such a percentage point in the polls, I always remember that it doesn't mean very much. I have seen worse and I have survived. I overcame those obstacles. You can't let yourself get distracted. On the Saturday following the announcement of my candidacy, the Gallup poll was not very encouraging, but it did not keep me from campaigning and talking about the things I cared about.

Among other things I talked about deficits and the public debt. It was Robert-René de Cotret, then President of the Treasury Board and a talented economist in his own right, who helped me prepare the economic aspects of my program. In it, we promised to balance the budget in four years by making a number of budget cuts. Taking into account the economic growth we foresaw and the impact it would have on government revenue, plus the reductions in expenditures, our calculations led us to expect to balance the books in four years. Kim Campbell, for her part, claimed it would take five years. The public, already very skeptical about politics, and the media saw only headline-seeking political one-upmanship in those predictions. Today, however, it has to be admitted that the Canadian government did manage to balance its budget in four years. I will never forget what de Cotret kept telling us: his analysis predicted that within four years the federal government would see its revenues exceed its expenditures by a wide margin. It was known, it was expected, and it is precisely what happened.

The other issue I took to heart in my campaign was the Youth Policy I had perfected when I was Minister of State for Youth. This was a unique opportunity to pick up on the ideas I had fought for in the past. If I won my bid for Prime Minister, I would have the needed authority to see those ideas implemented. This aspect of my program most captured the imagination of the delegates. Everywhere I went I repeated that we were going to initiate a policy that would enable every young person to be either in school, in a training program, in the job market or doing community work. I added that in order to reach that goal, I would change the unemployment insurance legislation, put that legislation at the service of provincial governments for purposes of training, and was prepared to adapt the legislation to the individual needs of each province. It was a new approach. People listened because the country was just coming out of a recession that had greatly affected some of their own children. They knew education was the defining issue for the future.

Meanwhile, Kim Campbell campaigned like someone who knew she was the front runner and wanted to avoid making mistakes. Nevertheless, she did experience her share of difficulties. There were five televised debates. I had the opportunity to verify something a friend had told me at the beginning of my leadership run. Campaigns of this kind, within political parties, can be very hard on individuals because they are a form of family feud. You witness things that illustrate the best and the worst about human nature. You see both extremes. All of a sudden, people with whom you think you share a deep friendship run out on you, and others, with whom you didn't think you had any great affinity, offer you their help and stick with you through thick and thin. Some of my Cabinet colleagues had everything to lose by supporting me. Yet they did, sincerely, because they believed in me, even though they were putting their futures on the line by doing so.

Conversely, others on whom I was counting for support, for all sorts of reasons, chose not to support me. During a leadership race, friendships are sorely tested. One of my closest friends was Pierre Blais. His decision not to support me was probably as hard on him as it was on me. We had so much in common. We enjoyed each other's company. I had been trying to reach him for several days to ask for his support while he had been off skiing with his children. By incredible coincidence we bumped into each other at the Toronto airport. It was six o'clock in the morning and each of us had just disembarked from a long night flight. The airport was deserted. We were both haggard and bleary-eyed. He had his family with him. We came face to face. It was as if fate had ordained that we should meet in that airport on that day. The conversation we had was very brief, even trite, and terribly sad. I asked him, "Are you going to support me?" He answered, "No." Fortunately for him and for me, time is a great healer and, after a while, we made up. It just shows how friendships can last. Even if you sometimes part ways as we did, the friendship, if sincere, will survive. Pierre and I have remained friends to this day.

In the case of Jean Corbeil, who was then Minister of Transportation, he had everything to lose by supporting me, but he did it anyway, as did Pierre Cadieux. My campaign turned into a classic underdog fight to the finish. The debates helped us a great deal. Strategically, as we needed to find ways to stand out, we looked forward to them. During the first English debate we could tell that Kim Campbell was not at all prepared—but I was.

In general, people tend to have a very simplistic view of debates. In reality they are a kind of cinéma-vérité. You don't go into one with the aim of delivering a knock-out punch. It is a serious mistake to begin a debate with the idea that you are going to flatten your opponent. It is better to concentrate on the message you think is important. If in the course of the debate you see an opening, you naturally seize the opportunity to tackle your opponent. But there may be no opening at all. It happens. Debates today are so scripted, so regulated that it has become very difficult to really score points against your adversaries. There is nothing magic about it, and it is not true that you debate the other side for three hours and everything is decided on the basis of one television clip. You must be prepared. You must know what you want to say. You must sufficiently internalize the subject matter to be able to speak spontaneously and, most of all, you must be yourself. You can't make it up as you go along. If the debates worked well for me, it was because I felt I was well prepared.

After Montreal and Toronto there was a debate in Calgary, which reminds me of a particularly tough break for me. Bernard Valcourt, whose backing I sought, called me just before the beginning of the debate to announce that he was not going to support me. His was a calculated, deliberate gesture, and it had an effect on my performance that night. It hit me hard. I lost my concentration just before going on stage. However, by the following debate in Vancouver, I had recovered and we carried on.

Photo-finish

When we arrived at the Ottawa convention, we had to face up to our situation. The reality was that we did not have the financial resources to compete with the Campbell camp. They spent almost 2 million dollars during that week alone whereas we spent a total of 2.2 million dollars for the entire campaign. But I knew the speeches could be the turning point. So, I put all my energies into preparing for the speech I was going to deliver in an environment that was completely new to me. I was appearing before an audience of eight thousand people, which is not the same as an audience of eighty or eight hundred. It can be a pretty intimidating experience the first time. When they make their speeches at the convention, the candidates' goal is to win over as many of the undecided delegates as possible. When the time came, my speech was very well received. We felt some real movement toward our camp from a significant number of delegates. But the next day, voting day, the die was cast after the first ballot. At the last minute, Jim Edwards, who had agreed to come over to my side if Kim Campbell failed to win on the first ballot, went over to her side instead. There was intense disappointment in our ranks. From the moment Edwards got up and started walking toward Kim Campbell I knew it was all over. But the people around me, especially Michou and Amélie, didn't necessarily realize the situation.

Between the first and second ballots I had a brief conversation with my campaign director, Jodi White, who said to me, "It's over. We have to find a way to tell Michèle. You can't tell her here, in front of everybody." Since it was very hot, some time had been set aside so I could go and change shirts. We decided that Denis Beaudoin would come along and tell Michou the bad news. We walked toward the room we had reserved and, while I was changing, Denis sat down with Michou and told her that it was over; we had to prepare to go back to the floor of the convention to await the result. Michou was very upset. She had kept her hopes up until the very last second. I said to her, "The people in our camp must not feel that it's over. First of all because you never know, and because, for them, it is very important. We have a responsibility for all the people who supported us, worked so hard, and believed in us. We have to be equal to the situation. We have to be able to get through this defeat with ours heads held high and not give in to bitterness. Those people don't deserve to come out of this with a bitter taste in their mouths. It is up to us to tell them that they can feel proud of what they did. Now it is time to turn the page. The sooner we do it, the better it will be for them, and for us."

So we plucked up our courage and went back to the convention floor. The results were announced. Kim Campbell won with 52.7% of the votes. A photo-finish. Then something unforeseen happened: We had completely forgotten to anticipate Amélie's reaction. She was ten years old and had insisted on being there that day. During the leadership race our children had not been present. We made that choice because we did not want to be seen as using them. Nevertheless, I was accused of exploiting my children, supposedly to distinguish myself from a childless Kim Campbell. Amélie had followed the race in the media and, on the last day, had absolutely insisted on coming with us. She had had a lot of fun, but, as we had forgotten to prepare her, when the result was announced she took it very hard. She didn't understand. Her dad had been "beaten".

Amélie was inconsolable. We will never forget poor Joe Clark sitting beside her and trying his best to comfort her as Michou and I made our way toward the stage. I have never seen the TV shot of her that people all over the country saw, but during the summer that followed I don't know how many times someone said to me, "I followed the leadership race. I was disappointed. I was hoping you would win, but you know, Mr. Charest, when I saw your daughter cry on TV, I cried too." I particularly remember one conversation in a store in Sherbrooke: An elderly lady approached me with her son, a big man in his forties who was at least 6 ft. 4. The lady explained to me that she had followed my campaign and was sorry I had lost. "Heavens, Mr. Charest," she said, "when I saw your daughter crying, I cried too." At which point her giant of a son, in a deep baritone, added, "Me too!"

Rude Awakening

When I later analyzed what had happened, I realized that all the no-shows at the beginning of the campaign had opened up the field. The problem you face in a leadership race is that everything is decided in the first weeks, not at the end. Once again the human factor in the process is critical. Once the delegates give their support to a particular candidate, they are loath to change their mind even if another candidate performs better in the campaign. They feel duty bound to their earlier choice. This is a noble human trait. If you decide to support me and another candidate later asks for your support, chances are you're going to answer, "I know you gave a better speech, and I know you've run a better campaign, but I gave my word." People consider their word important. Consequently, the best way to win in a leadership race is to secure a maximum of support right at the beginning. The first candidate to declare is the one who has the best chance of winning.

That was exactly what Kim Campbell did. When people said to me, "You needed just one week more," they were right. Except the week I needed would have had to come at the beginning, not at the end, of the campaign. What opened up the field for me, on the other hand, were all the big-name candidates in Ontario who decided one after the other not to run. In the early stages of the campaign, some delegates waited to see if those people were going to enter the race. This was why I was able to ask for their support. It is also why I was able to gain a foothold in unexpected places in a way that reflected Canadian values. In Alberta, for example, several people decided to support me because they liked my approach. When someone told them that a Québecer could not win because it was not his turn, because the leader had to come from elsewhere in Canada this time, they were offended. In the culture of Albertans, the idea that a candidate's value or destiny should be determined by their place of birth or social origins is unacceptable. "Some say I should support Kim Campbell," they would tell me, "because she is from the West, and that I should not support you because you are from Québec. Well I just don't buy that. If I support you, it's because you're the better candidate." For Michou and I the leadership race was a fascinating experience. It enabled us to really get to know the country. We made many friends—friendships forged in the heat of battle. It is one of the great secrets of political life. People who have not experienced it do not realize it. When you share such an intense experience with people, the friendships that result last a lifetime and can withstand anything.

The day after the convention, Amélie got up and informed me she didn't want to go to school. That is when I said to her the phrase that reminded me of my mother: "Well, I am going to the office this morning, and you are going to school, and life goes on." Still, the days that followed were not easy. In spite of my excellent advice to my own daughter, I can't say that I reacted very well. I was disappointed, of course, and I was bitter. I can remember going to a caucus meeting that followed the transition— I arrived late. When I think of it today, I do not feel very proud of myself. Instead of sulking, I should have made more of an effort.

With Kim, who from one day to the next had become Prime Minister, the discussions did not go well. She and the people around her insisted we meet the day after the vote. It was a mistake. We should have waited. It would have been wiser to speak on the phone and agree to meet a few days later. When we met for lunch the day after, I do not believe she was well-prepared for the transition and all that it entails, or to talk to an opponent who had come so close to winning and was very disappointed. At the end of that lunch I was furious. Our discussions concerning the role I hoped to play were off to a bad start.

I finally got over all that. Kim Campbell assembled her Cabinet. I was appointed Deputy Prime Minister, Minister of Industry and Science (a new ministry that combined the departments of Industry, Communications, and Consumer and Corporate Affairs), and Minister Responsible for the Federal Bureau of Regional Development for Québec (FBRDQ). I, therefore, had important ministerial responsibilities, but there was nevertheless a coolness, even a chill, in my relations with Kim Campbell.

Disaster

I went back to work. Unfortunately, I did not really have time to get to know my department. We were heading into an election. It was June and our mandate expired in the fall. During the summer, I traveled extensively in support of my colleagues across the country. I participated in numerous nomination meetings. I will never forget the typical media reaction, which was to ask, "Where is Charest? He has disappeared." The problem was that Charest was constantly on the road. I felt obliged to be. First, because I wanted to help my colleagues; second, because I was under close scrutiny within the Party.

I have heard it said that, in 1984, during the Cabinet meeting in which John Turner decided to call the election, Jean Chrétien, who had been Turner's close rival in the race to succeed Pierre Trudeau, had expressed reservations about going to the people at that time. Without divulging any State secrets, I too expressed strong reservations during our Cabinet meeting on the same subject. We were presented with a strategy that defined leadership as the central issue of the campaign. My reaction was very direct. I told my colleagues, "The issue of the next election is going to be jobs. If we want to talk about reducing the deficit to create jobs, fine; if we want to talk about leadership in terms of job creation, fine. But make no mistake. This campaign is going to be about jobs. Period." There was a long silence around the table, and a malaise, because the decision, evidently, had already been made.

There were going to be elections and there was disagreement between the Prime Minister and the Deputy Prime Minister. When Jim Edwards spoke up to say he agreed with me, the malaise only deepened. A discussion followed, during which I received a note from Jodi White, formerly my campaign director and currently Kim Campbell's chief of staff. "You have to conclude this meeting" was the substance of what she said. "Find a way to turn this around." I understood what she was asking of me. I made a plea in favour of Ms. Campbell. On my way out of the Cabinet meeting, I gave a scrum. Among the journalists was Jason Moscovitz, senior Parliamentary correspondent for the CBC. An insightful man, he looked at me and asked me one question in front of everybody. "What's wrong?" he asked. I asked him what he meant, forgetting that when someone follows you around every day for three months (Jason had covered my leadership campaign), they get to know your body language. Evidently, he detected my uneasiness. When I got back to my office I said to myself, "This is off to a bad start. We are going to have big problems."

The election was called the next day. Kim Campbell went to Rideau Hall, and from the very first day things began to go awry for her. Then I got a big surprise. I was Deputy Prime Minister and expected to participate in the campaign. But during the first two weeks, no one contacted me. No one asked me to do anything. I had invitations coming in from left and right, but there was no plan, no role for me coming from campaign headquarters. For the strategists, the situation was a little delicate. They were expecting Ms. Campbell to give them some direction about the role she wanted me to play. Since she said nothing, they concluded she was not comfortable with the idea of me participating too directly in the campaign. So, they made no move toward me.

After about ten days, we finally spoke up. "Listen," we said, "do you want us to do anything?" That is when the lights went on and we embarked on a campaign all across Canada. Once more, the media complained that I had disappeared. The reality, however, is that the media cover the leaders and no one else. They did not cover Paul Martin, on the Liberal side, any more than they covered me. During the last three weeks, I traveled constantly. In my own riding, the PQ and the Bloc published bogus polls claiming my seat was threatened. It wasn't, but it didn't make life any easier for me. The Bloc promised Québecers "*le vrai pouvoir*" ("real power") in Ottawa. Lucien Bouchard, speaking to the workers in the Bombardier plant at Sainte-Anne-de-la-Pocatière, dared to promise construction of a TGV (High-Speed Train) between Québec City and Windsor. When no one in the media questioned him on that statement, I said to Michou, "We're toast." Real Power? Would you like to order a High-Speed Train with that? And the leader of the Bloc Québécois was going to set it all up from the opposition benches! It was not the last time that Lucien would wave his magic wand to get votes.

Then came the infamous last week of the campaign. Ms. Campbell was forced to withdraw the horrible television commercials she made about Jean Chrétien. The next morning in the Montreal newspaper *La Presse*, there was an account of an interview she had given to the editorial board, in which she denounced me, Mazankowski, de Cotret and Mulroney. It was unreal. The election was a week away and she was publicly denouncing her own ministers and the outgoing Prime Minister—the man she had succeeded to the helm of her party. That same day, Jean Corbeil, another of her own ministers, one who had supported my leadership bid, wrote Ms. Campbell an open letter demanding she withdraw her statements. We couldn't believe it. We thought it couldn't get any worse, except we had yet to live through the day of the election. That day we were to learn that yes, things could get worse. We finished the campaign as best we could, but we were in very bad shape indeed. Toward the end I spoke with John Tory, the National Campaign Director, and asked him how many seats we could expect to save. He said he hoped for an even dozen.

The night of the election, October 26, 1993, we ended up with two seats in the whole of Canada: Elsie Wayne's in the Maritimes, and mine. To say we were in a state of shock is a gross understatement. That night Michou said to me: "Jean, you would have been better off losing. This can't be. Now you're trapped. You are thirty-four years old. You've been re-elected, but as for the rest, it's a disaster. What are you going to do now? If you had lost, at least we could have turned the page. You could have gone into the private sector and that would have been the end of it. But what is going to happen now? You can't leave. You've just asked the people of Sherbrooke to re-elect you." It was pretty depressing, but at the same time we had very mixed feelings. I had survived. It was a powerful moment because the people of Sherbrooke had voted for me. They had supported me in spite of everything. It was a vote of confidence and an extremely moving display of trust. I felt responsible toward the people who elected me. It was a determining factor in the choice I made regarding my own future. I also had a responsibility to my party, and, in the eyes of history, a duty to rebuild it.

The Only One Left

On my return to Parliament I remembered how, in 1984, we had looked down on those in the opposition ranks because they were Liberals. They had reigned for sixteen years only to be reduced to forty M.P.s. I had looked upon them with disdain, the forty who survived. We were so much better than them with our two hundred and eleven M.P.s. Now we were the dethroned—a majority government reduced to just two seats!

Elsie Wayne and I stood alone to represent the Conservatives. Of the one hundred and seventy Conservative M.P.s who had formed the previous government, I was the only one re-elected. All the others, including Ms. Campbell, had been defeated. Our last Cabinet meeting, right after the election, had an eerie feeling. All the ministers around the table, except me, had lost their seats. When I went with Michou to the last meeting of our caucus, we were given a warm welcome. I went around and shook hands with all of my colleagues. Of that group, I was the only one left in Parliament. All the others had been felled in the battle.

The Parliament of Canada was now polarized. On the one hand, there was the Bloc and the crypto-separatist Reform Party; on the other, the Liberal majority. There was now, officially, only one national party in Parliament. It was a very unhealthy state of affairs. For Canada to function properly, there has to be more than one party with a national vision inside Parliament. Where else can Canadians come together to discuss their common challenges? There have to be opposition parties that can offer constructive alternatives to the government policies they are criticizing. We need builders, not demolition experts. We need people who want to build more bridges between the different parts of Canada, not people who are going to devote themselves to blowing up the existing bridges. Throughout our history, Parliament is where those bridges between Canadians have been built.

We live in a country that demands a constant, ongoing effort in this regard. The Canadian tradition of seeking constructive compromise has shaped our history. It is one our country's great strengths. It stems from our geography and our linguistic and cultural diversity. We speak two official languages. We share two great cultures. And, as the West Coast turns towards Asia, Northern Canadians live and work in Inuktitut, Cree, Dene, and many other Aboriginal languages. To bring us together, to make the necessary accommodations between those different identities, we need Parliamentarians who believe in this country. It is too easy, in Canadian politics, to concentrate on what divides us. It is the solution preferred by demagogues. In the short term, it is the easy way to win votes. But a short-term political victory means nothing to me. Winning an election for the sake of winning is a meaningless exercise. If it is not to build a better society, to improve the lot of our fellow citizens, why get elected?

When I returned to Ottawa, I realized how hard political life can be. A few days before, we had been *the* government. We had made all the decisions. Now we were *persona non grata*. We were despised. All the places I used to go and where I felt at home had become foreign to me. They were full of strangers who now looked upon me with the same contempt I had shown toward the losing side in 1984. In the corridors of Parliament, I saw crowds of new Liberal, Bloc, and Reform M.P.s puffed up with pride, their noses in the air. In the Progressive Conservative Party we obtained 16% of the popular vote and only two seats. In contrast, the Bloc got 14% of the vote and landed 54 seats. Now they were the Official Opposition. That meant they would benefit from all the privileges that status confers, including the right to speak in the House and substantial research budgets.

A few days before the new government was sworn in, I ran into Jean Chrétien in a corridor of the Parliament buildings. He invited me to have coffee with him in his office. We had a pleasant conversation. I told him I would like to be able to keep the office I had on the fourth floor. He told me he did not think it would be a problem. But when it came to research budgets the government said no. As for the right to speak in the House during Question Period, again the answer was no. Every material and parliamentary means was being given to a party whose sole purpose was to break up Canada. And our party, one of only three parties in the House with a national vision, was being deprived of any and all resources, even though we had obtained 16% of the vote. It was undemocratic. Yet the more I protested, the more I realized how futile it was. In the minds of the public we had been turfed out and we deserved it. Too bad. Period. The reasoning was straightforward. The answer was always the same. People would say, "What is he complaining about? Doesn't he know we've just voted them out of office?"

The Progressive Conservative Party confirmed me as leader on December 14, 1993. That being said, the party was 10 million dollars in debt. The day after the election we had to lay off about ninety permanent employees, some who had been working for the party for thirty years. It was a very difficult task.

Muzzled

At the opening of Parliament on January 17, 1994, when Elsie and I arrived in the House of Commons, we discovered that we had been assigned seats far apart from each other. There was no valid reason for that. We had to fight tooth and nail to get the government to let us sit side by side in the House. It was a childish display of spite on the part of our fellow Parliamentarians. What could be the use of separating us if not just to rub salt in our wounds? I kept telling myself, "This is an unconscionable way to behave." Since the public had absolutely no sympathy for us, low blows were easy. It is something you never forget.

On the very first day, before the beginning of Question Period, the new Speaker of the House of Commons, Gilbert Parent, got up to announce that he had consulted the Whips of the three officially recognized parties and that Question Period was going to work in such and such a way. That was when I realized how cheaply my parliamentary rights had just been sold. In the parliamentary tradition, it is the Speaker's responsibility to represent the individual rights of each member of Parliament. But I had not been consulted. My rights had not been considered. Decisions on procedure had been made. Too bad for those who, by virtue of their number (we did not have the necessary quorum of 12), did not have official party status in the House and had to sit as Independents. In addition to Elsie and me for the Conservative Party, there were nine New Democrat M.P.s sitting as Independents. Our two parties combined had obtained 25% of the popular vote. One Canadian in four had voted for us, but it made no difference. We had been erased, blotted out. I protested, but to no avail.

Thirty Below

On the evening of the day the new Parliament sat for the first time since the election, I was to attend a fund-raising dinner in Kapuscasing in northern Ontario. During the campaign the President of the PC Canada Fund had promised, in the event the candidate for Kapuscasing was defeated, someone would be sent to participate in a fundraising event on his behalf after the election. Now, not only was I the only one of his former colleagues who had not been felled in the battle, but in the post-electoral context we were in, the only person, as leader of the Party, with any kind of drawing power. That being said, Canada is a big country. As there was no way that I was going to be absent from the House on the first day, I accepted the invitation on the condition that a charter be found to fly me to Kapuscasing right after Question Period and bring me back to Ottawa later the same evening. That winter was extremely cold. I had traveled extensively in the North on small chartered bush planes during the previous nine years and remembered to ask the person organizing the flight to make sure the plane's cabin was heated.

We took off from Ottawa flying against the wind. The pilot turned to me and asked if everything was okay. I asked him to turn up the heat and he gave me a thumbs-up sign. Half an hour later, while reading my notes, I

realized I was freezing. The engine was very noisy. It was
hard to hear. I tapped the pilot on the shoulder and he
gave me the thumbs-up sign again. Thirty minutes later, I
was even colder. The cabin had turned into a deep freeze.
I tapped the pilot on the shoulder again, and he again
signaled that everything was fine. The temperature kept
dropping so I tapped him on the shoulder again, and,
yelling to be heard above the noise of the engine, said,
"Turn up the heat! It's freezing back here!" He answered,
"But I have!" Finally he came to the back and checked.
The heater wasn't working.

Because of the headwind, the flight took two and a
half hours instead of one and a half. My left foot was
completely frozen when we landed in Kapuscasing. I could
not feel it at all. I got off the plane in the arctic cold.
People were waiting for me on the landing strip. I had
trouble walking. I went to the hotel where the event was to
take place. A room had been reserved for me. I settled
myself down, took off my shoes and socks and desperately
set about trying to thaw my feet. At that point a gentleman
came into the room. He went into the bathroom, took the
hair-dryer, and started blowing hot air into my shoes.
Meanwhile, I sat on my feet in an effort to warm them up.
Then several people filed in to shake the leader's hand. I
will never forget that scene. There I was, massaging my
feet with both hands. People came in. I stood up, barefoot,
and shook their hands while a volunteer was heating my
shoes with a blow-dryer.

We went to the meeting hall where the atmosphere
was friendly. A hundred people had braved the cold to see
me. You know you're not in the big city with the Ottawa or
Québec City press gallery when, after the scrum, the
journalists ask to have their pictures taken with you. Just
before I was to give my speech, a lady got up and came
over to my table. "Mr. Charest," she asked, "are you going
to speak soon?"

"Why yes, in a few minutes," I answered, "Why?"

"Well, I wanted to know when to start my car."

"Excuse me?"

"Well, yes. I just wanted to know when I should start my car."

She went back to her table, informed the people that I was going to speak soon, and then half the room got up and left. It was a little disconcerting, to say the least. When your speech is announced and half the audience walks out, it does not inspire confidence. I asked the person seated next to me what was going on. "You know," she explained, "it's so cold up here that if you start your speech now, an hour from now the cars will be warmed up." "But what about the other half of the room?" I asked. "Oh, their cars have been on since they got here!"

I delivered my speech. We had a good laugh. The people gave me a warm welcome. It was not the first time I noticed that in Canada, the colder the winter is, the warmer the people are. To show me how much they appreciated my coming to see them, they gave me a pair of beautiful fur mittens. It could not have been a more timely gift. I wore them for the entire flight back to Ottawa—on my feet! When I got home at around three o'clock in the morning, Michou was not impressed. "What are you doing? You start early... You get home late from your business in Kapuscasing..." I said, "Never mind. I have to warm up my feet." I remember getting to bed that night, completely frozen.

Bus Stop

Even though I was a party leader, I was a backbench opposition M.P. with no assistant, no car and no budget. One day when I was in my Sherbrooke riding office, an emergency called me back to Ottawa. I had to get back immediately. But I had no car. So, I told my riding office staff that I was going to take the bus. Here, you have to put yourself in their place. They were people who had recently gone from being part of the government, people whose party leader was the Prime Minister with everything that represents, to being people whose boss announces he is taking the bus to work. They insisted there was no way I was going to do that: "You're the leader of the Party," they protested, "you can't take the bus!" "Okay," I said, "so what would you have me do?" I phoned Michou in Ottawa to say that I was taking the bus home. She said, "You're just trying to make me feel guilty!"

I left Sherbrooke. The bus made a stop in Montreal and, as I had an hour's wait before the bus left for Ottawa, I decided to grab a bite to eat at the snack bar in the bus terminal. After a few minutes, two drunks came and sat down in front of me to watch me eat. One of them slurred, "I know you... Aren't you... Jean... Jean...?" Since I had often been on the news in the past year, people recognized me. I signed autographs for the taxi drivers and then boarded the bus to Ottawa. When I got there, I took a taxi home, went in and carried my bags upstairs to the bedroom. Michou was in bed reading. "Well?" she asked.

"Well what?"

"Well, what did you do?"

"Well, I took the bus."

"You did that just to make me feel guilty!"

"Non, no", I replied. "First of all, I'll have you know, dear, that I am very popular at the Montreal Bus Terminal." So Michou smiled at me and said, "Yeah. Well, don't let it go to your head."

Crossing the Desert

Purgatory lasted four years. In human terms, it was not a pleasant experience. Every day someone made a point of reminding me of my party's demise. Being the only Conservative re-elected to Parliament, I became solely responsible for all the ills for which the Party was blamed. In 1984-85 we, as a party, experienced the same phenomenon—only in reverse. Luckily, I very clearly remembered the "honeymoon" that followed our 1984 election. The human dynamic at work is very simple. An electorate that has just chosen a government does not change its mind the following year. It tends to be consistent and to want to validate the choice it has made. In its beginning, the new government can do no wrong. The public keeps finding reasons to forgive its mistakes. They give the new government a chance to prove itself. Related to that is an attitude, on the part of the newcomers, according to which everything their predecessors did is, by definition, wrong. In 1984, Pierre Trudeau was the worst calamity that had ever befallen Canada. Everything the Liberal Government had done prior to our election was bad, bad, bad. They did nothing good. Not one thing. Period. There was only us, and damn the consequences. Now the sheer scale of our defeat meant that we were to experience the same phenomenon even more acutely. All the problems that arose were entirely the fault of the Conservatives—end of story! And the fellow who now personified the Conservative Party was me.

All that had an impact on our troops, the rank and file members of our party. They were thoroughly demoralized. Under the circumstances, I went on a tour of the country for the sole purpose of reassuring them, of being there, of saying to them, "I am here. We are going to start over. We are going to rebuild, don't you worry." My message was simple: "We are the only national alternative to the Federal Liberals. As a government, we made some difficult and courageous decisions. History will be our judge. You have a right to be proud of what we did. In Canadian politics, the pendulum swings back and forth between the forces that divide us and those that unite us. This is not new in our history. Regionalism, from time to time, comes to the fore. It comes to the fore in the absence of a strong national vision. Regional interests take over when we do not have in our national Parliament leaders and parties capable of articulating a sufficiently inspiring national vision. It is the constant challenge of Canadian politics. You are continually put to the test. You are required to articulate solutions, to build the bridges necessary for our country to function. It is work that must be done consistently and without respite. Because as soon as you think the work is finished, people with a strictly regional vision will turn up. People who, in their own short-term self-interest, will strive to divide us." That was the message I delivered to the troops while at the same time trying to put things into perspective. The people had spoken. We accepted their verdict. Now it was time to roll up our sleeves. I would jokingly say, "They wanted to give us back our freedom. They may have exaggerated a bit, even a lot. But we have our freedom back; now we can rebuild the party."

I went back to fund-raising. The going was very tough during that first year. I had made a commitment to help all the defeated candidates who found themselves in difficult situations. These were people who had not seen the debacle coming and had expected to at least recover their deposit, i.e. to garner 15% of the vote in their riding. In Québec however, in two-thirds of the ridings, defeated M.P.s lost their deposits; in other words they could not, as the law allows, claim a refund for half of their allowable expenses. Their situation was disastrous. They were desperate. They had families to feed. From one day to the next they found themselves without work, penniless, in debt and calling out for help. The problem was that we were reduced to an army of one. When a riding association somewhere in Canada organized a fund-raising event, I was the only one who could travel. So my priority during that first year after the election was to help our people. From one end of Canada to the other I participated in as many events as I could. We changed the rules of party financing so defeated candidates could keep a larger share of the funds they managed to raise.

At the same time, I got down to the business of rebuilding party structures in order to make it the most modern of Canada's federal parties. I am proud of what we achieved and I am probably in a select group of ten or so people who are aware of everything we did. The fact is that no one paid any attention. The media didn't cover our activities and the public didn't care. Nevertheless, we rebuilt party structures from the ground up. The principles that guided us were democratization, openness and accountability. We produced a position paper and we organized a Party convention in April, 1995. We changed the method of choosing the leader. Having suffered from a delegate system that concentrated power in the hands of a few people in the party establishment, I wanted to open up the selection process to the members at the grass roots level.

The Party thus gave itself a system based on universal suffrage in which each party member gets to vote for the leadership candidate of their choice. We also redrafted the party constitution to make the leader accountable to the members and the members accountable to the leader. In the area of policy, we set up an open process based on consultation with the membership. All this work led to the Policy Convention held in Winnipeg in August, 1996.

I made up my mind to devote myself to rebuilding the party, so I decided not to attend the House of Commons. I could not be everywhere at once. Given that I had no budget and was not allowed to participate in House debates or to ask questions at Question Period, I had a role that was no more useful to play than that of an extra in a film. I had to decide what my priorities were. I said publicly that I was not going to attend the House; I was going to work at rebuilding the Conservative Party and serving my constituents in Sherbrooke; I promised to comment on proposed legislation even when I was not in the House. Nevertheless, I was hypocritically criticized for being absent from the House.

That being said, I could not have wished for a more devoted partner than Elsie Wayne. I used to joke that I shared my life with two women, Michou and Elsie. The latter had been mayor of St. John's, New Brunswick and a member of the Spicer Commission. She was a populist; that was the reason she had been elected. During the years that followed the election, she agreed to remain alone in the House of Commons to hold the fort and at least attend the debates even though she could not participate in them. It was very tough for her because there is nothing worse than being on your own in politics. Fortunately, our Conservative senators gave us a helping hand. In a way, they represented the only real opposition to the Chrétien government during those years.

Lucien Bouchard and the Bloc Québecois won their seats promising *"le vrai pouvoir"* to Québecers, but it was a farce. The Liberal government could pass any legislation it wanted. This was so true that the Chrétien government came to be the only government in Canadian history to actually enjoy Question Period. By definition, Question Period is the forum of the opposition. That is why it exists. It is not supposed to be a showcase for the government. Except that with the Bloc and Reform, it was so easy. The Bloc, in tandem with the PQ, which had formed the government in Québec City since September 1994, systematically indulged in provocation for the purpose of proving that Canada did not and could not work. Their job was to throw sand in the gears. But the government's answer to any question coming from the Official Opposition was easy: "Yes, yes, we know you don't agree, you can't possibly agree, you're separatists." End of story. The minister or Prime Minister would then sit down and that would be the end of it. As for the Reformers, they had no experience in the House with its rules and procedures, and they were very naïve in their approach to House debates. Theirs was a case of incompetence, pure and simple. They just didn't know what they were doing and they wasted an inordinate amount of time in the beginning just trying to understand what was going on around them.

The Liberals made the most of the situation. Because they had practically no opposition early in their mandate, they did not shy away from abusing their power. A good example is their use of gerrymandering both on the legislation that dealt with electoral boundaries and the bill they tabled on Pearson Airport. During the 1993 election campaign the contract to privatize Toronto's Pearson airport had been the object of intense debate. Right before the elections, the Conservative government had clumsily announced its intention to privatize the airport and had insisted on signing the contract during the campaign—big mistake. It was a gesture that invited all sorts of insinuations and allegations of wrong-doing. Jean Chrétien jumped on the opportunity to promise he would, if elected, cancel the contract.

To justify his decision, Chrétien's new government appointed Robert Nixon, a former leader of Ontario's Liberal Party, to inquire into the circumstances surrounding the privatization. He produced a report containing allegations of a very general nature—in other words a bogus report. That was the basis on which the new government canceled the contract at great cost to the Canadian taxpayer. The promoters sued, but the bill tabled by the government forbade them from resorting to the courts. It was unprecedented! It ran counter to the Canadian Charter of Rights and Freedoms. Nevertheless, the contract had been so decried by the Liberals during the campaign that no one took offense. The Bloc and Reform couldn't have cared less. The Minister of Justice, Allan Rock, defended the indefensible and no one in the public seemed to care. The Canadian Bar Association had to denounce the bill. It stated, categorically, in writing, that the bill was contrary to the Charter of Rights and flew in the face of the most fundamental rights of Canadian citizens. The government was finally forced to back down. It was the kind of situation that arises when a government has, for all intents and purposes, no opposition.

Toward a Referendum

Québec Premier Daniel Johnson called a general election in July, 1994. That day, Daniel had the courtesy to call me to tell me of his decision. From the very beginning of the campaign it became obvious that the leader of the Bloc, Lucien Bouchard, was damaging Jacques Parizeau's position rather than helping it. You could already sense the relationship between those two men was a difficult one. Bouchard even had to accept a more discreet role because his presence overshadowed and diminished Parizeau's stature.

The night of the election surprised everyone. Daniel Johnson, thanks to an extraordinary performance in the campaign, had succeeded in obtaining practically the same percentage of the popular vote as the PQ. He achieved this despite the fact that he had taken over the leadership of the Liberal Party of Québec in the dying days of its second mandate, a period of upheaval in the province marked by the failure of Meech, the Oka Crisis and the ravages of a major recession. The lack of a convincing victory to propel them into the referendum promised by Jacques Parizeau effectively raised doubts and discontent within PQ ranks to such a palpable extent that they were the subject of detailed analyses in the newspapers. The PQ campaign, in truth, gave short shrift to their pledge of holding a referendum on separation. The Péquistes, true to form, buried the separatist option to get themselves elected. They chose instead to focus on other, very negative themes. They attacked the government, promising *"l'autre façon de gouverner"* ("the other way to govern").

As soon as the péquistes, who were elected on a mandate of "good government", came to power, the entire government apparatus was thrown into high gear to prepare the ground for a winning referendum. This was the famous "third period" of Jacques Parizeau's referendum strategy. It followed the election of the Bloc in Ottawa in 1993 and the PQ in Québec City in 1994. In this regard, Mr. Parizeau had publicly committed himself to asking the clear question. "Do you want Québec to become a sovereign (or independent) country?" was how he had put it to journalist Michel Vastel a few months before the election[6]. In the same interview he expounded on the importance of clarity, recognizing that no one would be able to draw clear consequences from an ambiguous question. *"His watch-word: no more ambiguity ever"* (*"Plus jamais d'ambiguïté"*), was the subtitle of the article in *L'Actualité*. That was the position Jacques Parizeau defended until he again crossed paths with a certain Lucien Bouchard.

On the federalist side, we were on a war footing. The polls were beginning to outline a bedrock of support for each side; we could take for granted that 40% of the people were going to vote YES and 40% were going to vote NO. In other words, the 20% of the electorate who were undecided were going to decide the outcome of the referendum. The question then became who had the most credibility with that electorate. On the federalist side, my name surfaced most often in the polls. For the sover-

---

[6] See *L'Actualité* magazine, April 15, 1994.

eignists, it was Lucien Bouchard and Mario Dumont. Federalist strategists, recognizing the contribution I could make, expressed their willingness to see me participate in a referendum campaign. In preparation, I assembled a strategy team that included, among others, Senators Pierre-Claude Nolin and Michel Cogger, Jean-Bernard Bélisle, Jean Bazin, Claude Lacroix and François Pilote. We established lines of communication with the other federalist parties, i.e. the liberal parties of Québec and Canada in addition to my regular communications with Daniel Johnson.

During the summer of 1995, Daniel and I dined together in Montreal to talk about the referendum. We were beginning to define the strategy we would adopt. I told Daniel that for the purposes of the referendum, we could hardly put forward a concrete proposal that was going to get any kind of a fair hearing; the burden of proof had to be left with the sovereignists; we were not the ones proposing to separate Québec from the rest of Canada; we had to force them to demonstrate to the Québec population the validity of their secession project. At the same time we had to explain to Québecers the significance of voting NO, i.e. to link that option to a vision of the future that embodied the kind of society we wanted to build with other Canadians. But we faced a practical problem: The Prime Minister of Canada, Jean Chrétien, had been through the 1980 referendum when commitments had been made by Pierre Trudeau—commitments which, rightly or wrongly, were later perceived as having been broken. He had no wish to repeat the scenario. Politically speaking it was somewhat unfair: Now, Chrétien was Prime Minister and circumstances were different—but that was the situation we faced.

The Passport

In September, 1995, I went on a pre-referendum regional speaking tour: beginning in Sept-Îles; down to Baie-Comeau, where I delivered a speech before the local Chamber of Commerce; through Charlevoix in a cold rain; back to Montreal late in the night; up early to give a television interview. I caught a cold, got sick and lost my voice. The following week-end, I drove to the Beauce where the first major federalist rally was to be held. For several days I had been racking my brains to find a way of expressing what I believed was really at stake in the referendum. I asked myself the question: "In the end, what is the most precious thing we would be leaving behind if we ever decided to separate from Canada?" That was when the idea of the passport came to me.

The Canadian Passport is a powerful symbol. It represents an important component of our identity to which we are profoundly attached. It also symbolizes our place in the world and the reputation we enjoy. Without exaggerating the relatively modest role we play on the international scene, one can say that our influence, given our population (30 million) and our economy (only 4% of world GNP), is considerable. Why? Because we enjoy freedoms others do not have but dream of having. Thanks to the combined efforts of generations of Canadians, in Québec and all the other provinces and territories, Canada has become a country whose citizenship is one of the most sought after on the planet.

What is noble, what is great about Canada is the kind of society we have built in this country—a society different from any other. This is particularly true in the context of globalization. We stand apart because of our choices regarding language, culture and, most of all, values. We have a tendency to greatly underestimate our common values. Yet they constantly come into play in our daily lives. Freedom, democratic values, respect for differences, compassion and solidarity are values common to all Canadians—Québecers too identify with these values.

In the eyes of today's world our citizenship embodies these values. It would not have such value if not for the contributions made to it by French Canadians and Québecers. Our citizenship defines our relationship to our country and recognizes the diverse identities that make it what it is. They are not mutually exclusive. On the contrary, our citizenship is all the more precious because of the different identities it reflects. Diversity has always been a part of our reality and of who we are as a country. Since the beginning of our history we have been enriched by the coexistence among us of two languages and two cultures. There is absolutely no contradiction between being a Québecer and being a Canadian. There never was. Québecers do not perceive any contradiction between their identity and their citizenship. Only the most narrow-minded people claim to be unable to reconcile these two facets of our reality.

Can anyone argue that you cannot be a Montrealer *and* a Québecer? That you can't be a woman and a Québecer? That you can't claim Irish of Québecois origins? That you have to be one or the other? These are complementary aspects of who we are. That basic freedom of

Canadian citizenship is what is precious. We are free to be
a Townshipper, a Québecer and a Canadian, or to be an
Irish, francophone, Catholic Montrealer; the most precious
assets I possess are the ability to communicate in French
and in English and the access to two languages, two cultures, and two major world communities. Our citizenship
reflects this. For me, my children, Québecers and all Canadians, it is an instrument of freedom.

The freedoms expressed in our laws and in the
Charter represent formal expressions of a minimum below
which our society would cease to be a true democracy.
Actual freedom, as experienced in our daily lives, is what
allows individuals to find fulfillment and reach their true
potential. It is the freedom to learn more, understand
better and see farther ahead. It enables us to make better
choices and more informed decisions for ourselves and
our children. One of Canada's great strengths is the
freedom we enjoy that allows us the room to be different
from each other while sharing the same values. These
shared values—democracy, solidarity, tolerance, respect
for differences and the willingness to compromise—
constitute Canada's greatest strength. We may be a young
country, but we are nonetheless one of the world's oldest
democracies. Let us not forget it. The very vastness of our
country, with its small population, creates in every Canadian a need for solidarity for the sake of survival. We have
always needed one another. Canadian citizenship reflects
and symbolizes our partnership, our solidarity and our
common values.

Therefore, the passport was the perfect embodiment
of all we risked losing by voting YES. At the rally in the
Beauce, Lucienne Robillard, representing the federal government, Michel Bélanger, the president of our referendum committee and formerly co-chair of the Bélanger-
Campeau Commission, Daniel Johnson and I each spoke
in turn. When my turn came, bellowing to be heard because

of my lost voice, I reached into my pocket and took out a Canadian passport. The wild cheering that followed told me I had hit the bull's-eye.

The referendum campaign was officially launched at the beginning of October. It was to last thirty days. We gave it everything we had. Federalist spokespeople criss-crossed the province. From time to time we regrouped for a major campaign event. In preparation for the first large-scale federalist rally of the campaign, in Shawinigan—the Prime Minister's riding—in which he was scheduled to participate, my team debated if I should appear on the same stage as Jean Chrétien. The 1993 federal election was still fresh in their memories. It was a painful matter for Conservatives because partisan politics tend to make you resent your opponents. The situation had to be managed—quickly. I came to the conclusion that it was no time to let partisanship dictate our line of conduct. In that situation, our one and only over-riding interest had to be Canada.

The New Pilot

It was becoming increasingly obvious that the YES campaign was not gaining momentum. They needed to change their strategy—and they did so in spectacular fashion. Lucien Bouchard, without consulting Jacques Parizeau, bluntly announced to the media that a change in direction (a "*virage*") was necessary. The Premier of Québec, in extremis and no doubt in an effort to limit the damage that such a blatant lack of loyalty to his leadership might inflict on his organization, quickly complied with the dictates of his ally. He was soon to name Lucien Bouchard his "chief negotiator", in the event of a YES vote, for the negotiations that, he presumed, would follow with the rest of Canada.

In order to win over the greatest possible number of those dubbed by PQ strategists as "*les mous*"[7], the sovereignists recruited Mario Dumont[8] and concocted an "offer of partnership" (to be extended to the rest of Canada after a YES vote) that was either cynical or breathtakingly naïve. Even as it threatened a unilateral decla-

---

[7] Literally, "the soft".

[8] Mario Dumont: the leader of the Parti de l'Action Démocratique,which was founded in 1992 when he and Jean Allaire left the Québec Liberal Party in protest of Robert Bourassa's failure to formally adopt the Allaire Report.

ration of independence within one year if the negotiations with the rest of Canada did not go to their liking, the PQ regime was attempting to lead the population to believe, after a YES vote, it was going to be possible to calmly sit down over coffee and negotiate a "new partnership". They were, they assured us, going to discuss "calmly and serenely," with the "friendly country, our neighbour, our partner, with whom we have always lived[9]." It was utter nonsense. If those making such claims had just gone and tested the waters outside the province, they would have immediately realized that these assurances had no connection with reality. The sovereignist leadership obviously did not know Canadians in the other provinces very well, or else they were deliberately misleading Québecers to try to make them believe that such a major upheaval was going to be accepted without a ripple of protest. Did the stormy hearings of the Charest Committee and the Spicer Commission, or Meech and Oka not teach us something? Did these events not give us an inkling of what we could expect from one end of the country to the other ? Are those persons who forget their history not condemned to repeat it?

What struck me most, both about the threat of unilateral secession and the so-called "offer of partnership," was that the Péquistes, who love to wrap themselves in the mantle of democracy, were denying that after a YES in Québec there would be twelve other governments in Canada without a mandate from their constituents to negotiate anything at all. They refused to recognize that one of the foreseeable consequences of a YES vote in Québec would be that Canadians in the other provinces and territories would demand the same right as Québecers to determine their own future. To presume that "English Canada" was a homogenous bloc was naïve, not to say

---

[9] See in particular Lucien Bouchard's speech at Verdun, on October 25, 1995.

ignorant, in the extreme. The regions of Canada are very
different one from the other. Where we all find common
ground is with regard to our values. The PQ clearly understood this, as even their rhetoric, centered on the Canadian
dollar, the economic union, and the Canadian values of
tolerance, compassion and solidarity, amply demonstrated.

Another favourite argument in favour of separation
was that "we" Québecers were different. To be different,
according to them, meant that we could not live with "the
others." By the same token, Jonquière and Chicoutimi[10]
should not be in the same country. When you know the
rivalries that exist between Montreal and Québec City, the
pretext of "difference" does not hold water. To me, that
argument is repugnant. We have devoted too much energy
and creativity to building a country based on the respect
for differences to just break it up and build another one
based on uniformity just beside it.

[10] The turf-wars between these two neighbouring municipalities are legendary.

Verdun

Six days before the referendum, the federalist forces gathered at the Verdun Sports Arena. It was the day the markets had reacted negatively to the latest poll showing the YES and NO sides in a dead heat. The change in the atmosphere was palpable. Around the sports complex, all the streets were blocked. Traffic was at a standstill. I was impatient, exasperated. I said, "I've had enough. Let's walk," and I got out of the car. Walking along the street I saw Prime Minister Chrétien and his wife Aline ahead of me, also getting out of their car. We exchanged greetings and began to walk together. On the way, people stopped to say hello to him so I told him the old joke that Camillien Houde, a famous Montreal mayor, had told the Queen. I said, "You know, some of those people are greeting you too!" He had a good laugh. When I entered the arena it was packed to the rafters. Outside, a throng of people who had not been able to get in waited in the rain to watch the proceedings on giant screens. When the speeches began, the crowd went wild. I had never seen anything like it. Daniel Johnson spoke first. I followed. When I give a speech I like to be spontaneous. The challenge is to capture the moment. When I am in contact with people in the audience before the speech it inspires me. I began by saying the

Prime Minister and I had bumped into each other on the way in and that we had walked together. Whatever the circumstances, wherever I might be, whatever our political allegiances, I said that when it came to preserving Canada for Québecers, he and I would always walk that road together. That night, the Prime Minister, in response to the appeal Daniel Johnson had publicly made to him a few days before, made a number of commitments including recognition of Québec's distinct character and restoration of the constitutional veto. I pledged to act as the guardian of those commitments.

Danger Signs

A few weeks earlier, a big federalist rally with members of the business community was held at the Palais des Congrès in Montreal. They were 3000 strong and we could feel how eager they were to publicly express themselves. They came to tell their fellow Québecers how much they wanted Canada to succeed, and how much they wanted Québec to succeed within Canada.

I left right after my speech that night. I had a plane to catch. I was bound for Chicoutimi where I was scheduled to participate in a debate to be held in a building called "La Vieille Pulperie," and televised on the Radio-Canada public affairs program *Le Point.* I was happy to be going back to that building because I had sponsored its renovation when I was Federal Minister of the Environment (responsible, at the time, for historic sites and monuments, and for the Federal Bureau of Regional Development for Québec). As Deputy Prime Minister in the Campbell government, I made the necessary funds available to carry the project through to completion. Also appearing on the show that night were Liberal MNA Liza Frulla and, for the sovereignist side, PQ MNA Jacques Brassard and ex-labour union activist Monique Simard.

When Michou and I arrived on the set we immediately sensed the tension coming from the invitation-only audience. The debate, moderated by journalist Jean-François Lépine, was relatively civil, except that during the commercial breaks people in the crowd shouted abuse at Liza Frulla and me. When the debate ended, the expressions of hostility from the sovereignist side of the audience continued unabated with an intensity that I had never seen in an election campaign. Upon leaving the hall, Michou and I, for the first time in our lives, narrowly escaped being physically assaulted. There was no security on hand to intervene. François Pilote, my assistant, came to our rescue. Michou was very shaken. That was the first time in my ten plus years in politics we had ever felt threatened at a public event.

Toward the end of the campaign, the public debate degenerated to a disturbing extent. We all still have in our minds the declarations concerning "money and ethnic votes" made by Jacques Parizeau on referendum night. However, there had been others during the referendum campaign. It is sufficient to remember the big sovereignist rally of October 25th at the Verdun Arena. The referendum was five days away. Passions were at their peak. Instead of acting responsibly, in a statesman-like manner and calming the crowd, Bouchard poured oil on the fire. The only conclusion you could draw from his tirades and the reactions they provoked among too many of his sovereignist supporters was that their secession project was motivated by anger and resentment. It was not founded on a generous and constructive vision of the future but on a settling of accounts with enemies, "traitors", whose worst sin lay in not thinking as they did.

Despite their campaign billboards depicting daisies or the peace and love symbol borrowed from the 1960s "love generation", the sovereignist campaign was essentially negative. In its anti-federalist propaganda the YES camp banked on the economic situation: Canada's deficit and over-all debt had prompted severe criticism from the *Wall*

Street Journal. The Péquistes claimed Canada was bankrupt. "Better to leave the ship before it sinks," they warned. They were trying to promote the illusion that the people had nothing to lose by leaving Canada. They unscrupulously exploited a set of economic circumstances to argue that sovereignty was going to solve every problem. Who can forget that Lucien Bouchard, during the referendum campaign, went so far as to say that a YES vote would have the same effect as waving a "magic wand"? In spite of Québec's huge deficit, which the Campeau Budget put at 5.7 billion dollars, Lucien Bouchard and Jacques Parizeau both claimed that a YES would protect Québecers from budget cuts—the so-called "cold wind from the West" that was "sweeping" the English-speaking provinces and "threatened", we were told, to devastate Québec. In reality—as could be seen from an article by journalist Denis Lessard that appeared in *La Presse* on October 20th, 1995, i.e. during the referendum campaign—top civil servants in Québec City were preparing for draconian cuts to the budgets of all government departments immediately following the referendum, whatever its result.[11]

---

[11] See "Québec devra bientôt serrer la vis—Des lendemains budgétaires difficiles après un OUI ou un NON", *La Presse*, Octobre 20, 1995.

50.4%

Referendum night is forever branded in our memories. With 50.4% of the vote, we won, but we almost lost the country. That night, we were treated to Jacques Parizeau's awful rant blaming "money and ethnic votes" for the defeat of his option. When you are in politics you don't have the right to say anything that goes through your head—even at the most painful moments. You are speaking, first and foremost, on behalf of others—the people who elected you. It is a heavy responsibility. Jacques Parizeau was Premier of Québec, and, on the night of October 30, 1995, he was speaking on behalf of all Québecers.

The close referendum result guaranteed that the Péquistes would return to the attack. It also reminded us of the limitations inherent in a referendum held in a modern democracy. There are some who think a referendum is *the* answer. This is notably the case with Péquistes and Reformers. But, as a solution to the complex problems that arise in a democracy, it is, inevitably, simplistic. A modern democracy cannot be reduced to a simple mathematical formula where you count votes, that's it, that's all. In a true democracy we have to be able to take into account minority opinions. That is the essence of a modern democracy. It is the reason why no one in Canada contests the right of a Québec government to hold a referendum on secession. Canada is at the forefront of the world's democracies precisely because it accepts dissent.

Canada's performance at the Earth Summit in Rio is a good example of the democratic spirit I am describing. The positions Canada adopted took into account the opinions expressed by all the members of the Canadian delegation, including those whose opinions differed from the government's. Instead of excluding them from the process, we included them, consulted them, and gave them their say. This does not mean we always agreed with them, but we gave them a chance to persuade us and we in turn did our best to persuade them. This kind of experience is a good illustration of the real challenges inherent to democracy. It is a far cry from Jacques Parizeau's famous "lobster" analogy[12]. Real democracy also requires democratic parliamentary institutions and governments to share information with opponents. The real challenge facing men and women in politics today is not so much winning as persuading. True democracy requires access to information, not propaganda.

Some think power means you can do whatever you want—in reality, the very opposite is true. The advantage of power is the privilege of setting the agenda. But from that point on there are only obstacles. And for those who chose to disregard dissident opinions, the obstacles rapidly become insurmountable. Much has been made of the accepted democratic standard that says a referendum on secession can be "won" with 50% + 1 of the votes. The reality is that a public consultation like that, in which the YES side prevails by just a small fraction of the vote,

---

[12] A reference to a comment made by Jacques Parizeau at a meeting with foreign diplomats a few months before the 1995 referendum, to the effect that once Québecers voted YES, they would be like "lobsters in a pot", i.e. there could be no turning back.

instantly creates a divided society. The Québec population would be torn in two, polarized, deadlocked. From then on, how could we build? And what would we build? And for whom? We have to stop perpetuating these divisions among ourselves. It is time to recapture the common will that enabled us to build Québec within a country that embraces diversity—a country called Canada.

"Who are You?"

Jacques Parizeau was forced to resign the day after the referendum because of the statements he made the previous night. Lucien Bouchard, as expected, soon replaced him as leader of the PQ and Premier of Québec. In the House of Commons, Prime Minister Chrétien quickly decided to table resolutions on the recognition of Québec as a distinct society and the veto. I had the opportunity to meet with him at his official residence at 24 Sussex Drive. I was against the idea of tabling those two resolutions not because I was against recognizing Québec as a distinct society—I had already voted in favour of such a measure in the House of Commons several times in the past—but because I felt a lot still needed to be done to build a national consensus on the issue.

So I recommended to Mr. Chrétien that he not act with undue haste. I said that he should first take the time to persuade Canadians both in Québec and the other parts of Canada. Mike Harris expressed the same reaction for essentially the same reasons. I said to the Prime Minister, "If you do it now, you are going to polarize the country. You are going to give a weapon to Preston Manning," whose opposition to the idea of distinct society was well known. "He will use it against you and everyone else, and it will only poison the debate even more." I added that we would do well to stand back, rebuild the bridges between Canadians and focus on changes in favour of which a consensus already existed, particularly regarding the economy.

The advantage of such an approach was that it would allow him to act immediately and set the table for future constitutional change at an appropriate time. Among other things, I stressed that what was needed was a rebalancing, a redistribution of responsibilities to start putting it into practice. I also suggested to Mr. Chrétien that he convene a First Ministers Conference with the aim of forging a consensus on the issue of deficits and public debt so that governments could agree on some common objectives. I argued that such an approach would have the added advantage of giving the more recalcitrant provinces some political support for their efforts at rationalization. Finally, I said it would enable the federation, and the way it worked, to evolve.

However, Prime Minister Chrétien then interpreted the outcome of the referendum as a mandate to have Québec recognized as a distinct society. It was what he had pledged and he decided to table a motion in the Commons to that effect, along with a bill providing for a regional veto. The veto immediately ran into problems when British Columbia demanded to be considered as a region in its own right—distinct from the Western provinces. There was a debate in Parliament about the Prime Minister's referendum promises. I still did not have the right to speak in the House. However, when the time came, the Liberals agreed to let me take part in the debate. The Bloc and the Reform Party, on the other hand, were categorically opposed. So I swallowed my pride and went to see Michel Gauthier, who had just succeeded Lucien Bouchard as leader of the Official Opposition, to ask him if he would agree to my participation in the debate. I shall never forget his answer. He eyed me coldly and said, "Who are you?"

Thus prevented from taking part in Parliamentary debate, I realized that I was wasting my time in the House of Commons and re-immersed myself in the rebuilding of the Conservative Party. In the other provinces of Canada, the reaction to the Québec referendum result was highly emotional. The feeling of despair, even of resentment toward the political leadership, remained palpable for many months. People could not accept having come so close to losing the country and they were determined to never let it happen again. It was a gut reaction, a cry of despair from Canadians who did not want to have to relive such a traumatizing experience. This was the atmosphere in which the Supreme Court Reference was initiated. From the beginning I expressed my disagreement with that initiative. The Courts are no substitute for the common will to share the future—a will that has held us together through our entire history.

The Young Take the Floor

Although I had been in the public spotlight for several weeks, the day after the referendum I knew I would soon disappear from view again. My participation in the campaign did, however, have a positive effect on my efforts to rebuild the Conservative Party. For the first time in a long while, rank and file members of the Party had reason to feel proud of a contribution we had made to the public debate. It was important because it presented an alternative, a different vision of the country to build on. They were galvanized and, anticipating a federal election early in 1997, we began to prepare. In August, 1996, we held a Policy Convention in Winnipeg to put together the framework of our election platform. The Young Conservatives, like the Young Liberals in Québec, were well-organized, well-represented within the Party, and very militant. They always stood to the right of the Party leadership on the issues. As it happened, the Ontario Conservatives under Mike Harris had been elected the year before by advocating major changes in the way the province was governed. Their influence could be felt within our own Party.

At our policy convention, the Young Conservatives initiated a strong movement in favour of reducing taxes.

These young people and their peers across the country expressed a heartfelt concern about their future. It is a serious mistake to seek to reduce the issues they raised to simplistic notions of "right" and "left". They were registering their discomfort with the way we governed ourselves, the choices we made, and the fact that we made no room for them in our society. They reminded us that the State is an important player that influences the choices people make. When it came to the public purse, they were acutely aware of the fact that they were going to have to pay for the mistakes made by others before them. That is an injustice we cannot afford to simply sweep under the rug. They were introducing a new and legitimate element to the debate, one based on the idea of fairness between generations. At the Winnipeg Policy Convention, it was the young people who persuaded a sufficient number of party members to accept the validity of their arguments, a feat which obliged the Party to commit itself to tax reduction. I was comfortable with that consensus. I agreed with the conclusion not for ideological reasons but because of my own analysis of Canada's economic situation.

What I believe now, as I did then, is that a government that takes 50% of our earnings is at cross purposes with our economic environment. From a historical perspective, every generation has seen people leave Europe and other parts of the world to come to North America in search of the economic freedom they could not find elsewhere. In that sense, Québecers are profoundly North American. In other words, we all have certain economic expectations. We believe we have the right to work, and to work as hard as we wish. We also believe we have a right to enjoy the fruits of our labours. This belief is entirely compatible with our concern for social justice; one does not contradict the other. During the last thirty years, Québec governments of all political stripes, in their efforts to narrow the gap between our standard of living and those of our neighbours, lost all sense of proportion to the point where we are now the most highly taxed jurisdiction in North America.

The net effect of that hard reality is that the most productive, ambitious people leave the province to live, work, invest and pay taxes elsewhere. It is an implacable law of the market that has to be understood, accepted, and, above all, reconciled with our concern for social fairness. It will require of governments a major readjustment in the way they administer our public finances. This has implications for the federal government too. It should be noted that other federations in the world are subject to the same pressures as Canada. In the United-States, where people are equally concerned about public finances, the debt accumulated by past governments and over-taxation, a similar debate concerning the relative roles of the federal and state governments is underway. In other federations the roles of the different orders of government are being re-examined, as are the responsibilities they have taken on. Good decisions can be made only on the basis of estimates that are objective and accurate, but to these questions the Parti Québecois offers only the simplistic solution of eliminating one order of government. However, in the United-States, to cite but one example, three orders of government exist: the federal, state and municipal governments. This arrangement does not keep the U.S. from functioning.

The adjustment that has to be made is in the roles assigned to each level of government. This has to be done in a way that ensures each is equally accountable. Accountability is a very important rule of democracy. Citizens have to know who is responsible for what. The electorate has to know what level of government is responsible for what decision so it can be held accountable. Responsibility, in personal as in political life, is important. The people who vote and pay taxes have the right to know who makes the decisions and who does what with their money. Democracy works to the extent that responsibilities are as clearly defined as possible. The more accountability there is, the more likely it is that our governments will make good decisions. An added new factor is that more and more of the problems we face do not fit neatly into any one jurisdiction. If we approach them in a narrow legalistic manner, we will never be able to solve them. What we have to learn to do is to set common objectives and then let each order of government, in its own sphere of responsibility and in keeping with its role, contribute to achieving those objectives. That is one of the future challenges of federalism.

That was the spirit in which our election platform proposed a new covenant based on the notion of co-management and co-decision. On tax reduction, our proposals were centered around job creation. In a modern economy, the places where jobs are created are the places where taxes are lowest. Those are the economies that attract investments and productive people. The sooner we understand that in Québec, the sooner we will be able to create and redistribute wealth instead of poverty.

Difficult Decisions

We began to prepare for the campaign we knew was approaching. A period of intense activity followed. I devoted myself to the recruitment of candidates to run for the Party in the election. This is not an easy task when you are the leader of a party of only two M.P.s. It was even harder when it came to recruiting women. Many women do not identify with the political environment. Question Period does not interest them. It leaves them cold. When I was a minister I sometimes asked Michou, when I got home, whether she had watched Question Period on television. Her responses were seldom enthusiastic.

"You really liked your answer today, didn't you?" she would merely remark.

"Yes, I thought it was pretty good…"

"It showed," she would quip, "that you really liked your answer today."

Needless to say, she brought me back to earth. This does not mean that we should underestimate the importance of the role played by parliaments and legislatures in forcing governments to show a minimum of accountability. It protects us against the abuse of power.

In recruiting candidates for the election, we were looking for men and women who were well-balanced and well-rooted in their own communities. The kind of political representation I would wish upon any population is not necessarily the most brilliant thinker or the most eloquent speaker: The most important thing to remember is that we are elected by people who expect us to represent them and defend their interests. There is something very healthy about an M.P. or M.L.A. who takes to heart the interests of his or her constituents. It is good for democracy.

In our search for candidates we recruited many young people, which was encouraging. And we almost erased our debt. But our big challenge was to define our expectations for the outcome of the election. Given that we were a political party whose scope was nationwide, we did not think it appropriate to say that our objective was to win twenty or forty seats. For a national party, the aim is always to replace the government. This created such high expectations that, in the end, it did not serve us well. Our real problem was one of critical mass. Even after the debates, after we had managed to capture the attention of the electorate and get our message heard, when the time came for voters to make their choice, the fact remained that we were a party with only two M.P.s. After the leaders' debates, sensing that we now had the wind in our sails, our opponents exploited this theme relentlessly in an effort to prove that I could not form a government. "Where is his team?" they asked. Even though we recruited men and women who had integrity and were willing and able to serve their country, we still lacked credibility.

To me, the most striking event of the 1997 federal campaign has to be the decision by Preston Manning to deliberately whip up the anti-French/anti-Québec sentiments of a minority of voters who form the hard core of the Reform Party. His televised campaign ads unscrupulously exploited post-referendum resentments for the sole purpose of polarizing the electorate. Intransigence is the worst trap into which we can fall and one Canadians must resolutely avoid. It is why we need parties that are national in scope—parties that are obliged to include and reflect all the regions of the country. The opposite leads us to polarization, a harmful dynamic that feeds on ignorance and mutual prejudice.

I made some difficult decisions during that campaign: among them was defending the idea of Québec as a distinct society, which we included in our program. We knew very well that, in Western Canada, this position would make us the target of the Reform Party that opted for a very negative "American-Style" strategy. It consisted in identifying "hot-button" issues and exploiting them without scruple. Tactics like these are very divisive, but they can be effective. I was not about to retreat before such an offensive and it must be said that our three hundred and one candidates, to their credit, defended our Party's position on distinct society in every part of the country. They did so lucidly, knowing full well that it was unpopular. It was to cost us dearly.

Another difficult decision I made was to answer Manning's ads unequivocally. I called him a bigot in an effort to shake up those people in the Ontario electorate who might have been tempted to vote for Manning. I knew we were not going to benefit, but we stopped the Reform Party at the Ontario border. They lost the only Ontario seat they had managed to win in 1993. But our candidates in Western Canada paid a heavy price. It was to be expected and they accepted it without complaint.

The 1997 campaign was difficult for another reason: Before the election, Manning announced he would send Reform Party members to each of our public meetings to heckle us. Everywhere we went, Reformers followed, heckling and trying to disrupt the proceedings. During one campaign stop at an Ontario shopping mall, violence erupted. Two people ended up in hospital, one a young girl who suffered a concussion. Amélie was with us that day. She was terrified.

You Have One Minute!

The leaders' debates helped us considerably. Once again, what works in a televised debate is authenticity. You have to be well prepared and know what you want to say, but, above all, you have to be yourself. And you have to listen closely to what your opponents are saying so you can reply at the right moment. For instance, during the English debate when Jean Chrétien, on the subject of public finances, said that thanks to his government we were finally seeing the light at the end of the tunnel, I spontaneously shot back, "The light you see is the whites of the eyes of the electorate." That said, the debate formula has its limits. For example, the part of the French debate that dealt with national unity had to be restaged because the moderator, Ms Claire Lamarche, suddenly collapsed. We were later reassured as to her condition, but at the time we were very concerned.

When the debate finally resumed each candidate was allotted a total of only ten minutes, and we each had only one minute for our closing remarks. I will never forget the media commentary that followed. "My goodness," analysts complained, "those people have nothing to say." The question we were asked was something like, "How do you foresee the future of Canada in the global context?" In short, solve the problems of the world for us: you have one minute to do it and if you don't succeed then you have nothing to say!

Our children, Amélie, Antoine and Alexandra, were fascinated by the debates. The following day they always wanted to know all the news. One image in particular sticks in my mind: As I was driving them to school, I turned around and saw the tops of three heads buried in three newspapers held open in front of them... There is no doubt that the debates allowed me to score some points, a fact to which my opponents' reactions testified. The problem was that, on the ground, we were not well prepared to manage our own success. Eventually our campaign ran out of steam. Statements made by the Prime Minister to the effect that he would not accept a result of 50% + 1 in a referendum on secession polarized the vote in Québec just as we hit the credibility problem I mentioned earlier.

The results of the campaign were disappointing. Nevertheless, we succeeded in winning thirteen new seats in the Maritimes, one in Ontario and five in Québec, which were concentrated in the Eastern Townships except for one in the sovereignist heartland of Chicoutimi that we owed to André Harvey's superb campaign. I was all the more pleased as Michou and I know the Saguenay-Lac-Saint-Jean area well. Michou had taken a keen interest in the Vieille Pulperie renovation project during my stint as Minister of the Environment. We both love the artists, painters and sculptors of that beautiful region. As Minister, I supported a project to move the house of the painter Arthur Villeneuve. The entire structure, its every nook and cranny, is a work of art in itself. Prior to the election we held a big rally—twelve hundred people—in the area for André Harvey, a courageous man who had sacrificed a great deal to return to politics. He took an enormous risk, and won. André Harvey is a first-rate representative of the people—the kind you would wish on any population.

A Time to Reflect

The summer of 1997 was a time for me to take stock. Several people close to me had strongly advised me to move on. They said I had done my duty to my country and my party. They argued that at my age, thirty-nine, the time was right for starting a new career and that I could always go back into politics some day. My family was also telling me it was time to consider my future. The night of the election, Michou and Amélie came to see me as soon as the results were announced. They were upset and asked me to resign. Amélie, who was fourteen, did not mince her words: "Daddy", she said, "I've had enough. Tonight, it's time to go. You've done enough. I want you to announce tonight that you're leaving!" I was stunned. Amélie, like Michou, had gotten very involved in the campaign. Amélie in particular had come to know some women candidates of great worth whom she admired. She became attached to them and did not take kindly to their defeat. Her disappointment was intense and she wanted me to resign immediately. Her fear was that if I let a few days go by, my responsibilities would reclaim me to the point where I would not be able to leave. That night I told her no. However, I promised to take the summer to think about it.

We vacationed in Italy with the children. The first week, while in Tuscany, the subject came up again. We were eating outdoors when Michou started the conversation with the children. "It's time we thought about our future," she said, "and it's time we made some decisions." Alexandra, our youngest, who at that time was seven years old, had a completely unexpected reaction. When she realized what we were deciding—whether I was going to stay in politics or do something else—might mean moving to another city, she cried, "I don't want to go and live somewhere else!" and burst into tears. "I don't want to leave my friends! I don't want to go somewhere else!" she kept repeating through her sobs. Michou and I were physically and mentally exhausted. Neither of us wanted to launch into a debate that was going to be as intense as this one promised to be. We didn't mention the subject again. We visited churches, palaces and museums, in Florence, Luca, Pisa, Rome and Venice. We went to Paris for one wonderful week. When we returned to Canada after four weeks, we still hadn't made a decision.

Parliament was about to resume. Our caucus had to be prepared. Even though we won just twenty seats and ranked only as the fifth party in the House of Commons, we made enormous progress. We regained official party status, the right to speak in the House, and a budget for operations. And I was no longer alone. I now found myself among colleagues, people to talk to and with whom to share my dreams. Now, when I stood up to speak in the House, the Bloc and the Reformers would boo and heckle me—a sure sign of improvement! On a more personal note, I found the capital becoming a more friendly place.

During the Fall, Michou and I talked about our future. The people around me could feel me hesitating and they pressed me to make a final decision, a decision that would have a number of implications. Indeed, if I decided to stay on, I would want to see to consolidating my leadership and, above all, get on with rebuilding the Party. I was also going to have to assert my presence in

Parliament. Meanwhile, my own M.P.s were telling me in caucus that they sensed a hesitation on my part. When you are the leader of a party you have a responsibility to your troops.

Everything finally came together around our decision to buy a house in Ottawa. The house in Hull where we had lived for twelve years had become too small for our growing family. We were happy with the life we had. One of our great successes as a family was the stability we managed to give ourselves. Michou had a circle of friends, couples our own age who were not involved in politics. So, we decided to buy a house on the Ottawa side of the river to be closer to our children's school. Such decisions matter in the everyday life of a family. You buy your first house. Your family outgrows it. Your children are two to a room. So you buy a bigger house. It's the house you settle into for keeps. Once we made the decision to by the new house, I assembled my principal collaborators and told them, "I'm staying."

The Call

On March 2, 1998, Daniel Johnson decided to retire from politics; it changed our lives completely. Michou and I were in Toronto preparing to leave for an eight-day tour of Western Canada when he made his announcement. We realized the impact of Daniel's decision when a crowd of reporters showed up for a speech I was giving before the Greater Toronto Real Estate Agents Association. Their interest in me was so great that I had to give a scrum at my hotel that afternoon to say that I had no intention of applying to succeed Daniel Johnson. That night, on returning from a dinner, Michou and I found my assistant waiting for us in the hotel hallway with a message from Amélie asking that I call. "Madame," he said to Michou, "she specified that she would like her father to call her back, not her mother." We went into our room and I called home. Amélie answered and the first thing she asked me was whether I was calling from a " land" phone (as opposed to a cellular phone). In other words she wanted to know if I could speak freely. I told her I could, that I was calling from the hotel. "Good," she continued. "Now I want to know what's going on, and I don't want you to give me any *spin*," which in political jargon means the official version. I told her what I knew. She listened intently and said, "Okay. Tomorrow morning before I go to school, I would like to have the newspapers and a copy of your schedule." Even though she was only fourteen, she had enough experience to know that by reading my schedule she would be able to decode who I was seeing and have an idea of the probable turn of events.

From the first day I declined the invitation to come to Québec to replace Daniel Johnson as leader of the Québec Liberal Party. But I could not foresee the extent or the intensity of the reactions that were to come from all sides, mostly from Québec but also from other parts of Canada. During my trip through the West I got a very strong sense that the people wanted a leader in Québec who could, and would, bring the different communities together. That was something they had in common with many Québecers: A desire for someone who could build bridges and express everything that it is possible to do together, within a united Canada; someone who would be capable not only of setting the objective but of reaching it.

From Québec it was a real *cri du coeur*. It came in the form of phone calls, telegrams, letters, faxes and e-mail. I would call the office and my staff would tell me that they were being inundated; they had never seen anything like it. The telephone was ringing off the hook at the riding office, my office on Parliament Hill, at the Party office and the leader's office. Messages were flooding in from all sides. No matter how many times I repeated that taking the helm of the Québec Liberal Party was not a possibility I was considering, people would not accept it.

Finally, after eight days, I returned to Ottawa. The children were eager to see me. We had dinner together, just the five of us. I told them there was going to be a meeting of the caucus the next morning, and I and our M.P.s were going to announce that I would consider the invitation I had received to take the leadership of the Québec Liberal Party. Once again, it was Alexandra who set the tone. She started crying and disappeared under the table. That lasted about ten minutes. I can see myself now, standing, bent over the corner of the table, trying to persuade her to come back to her seat. "Alexandra, we can't talk if you are under the table." "No!" she cried. I won't come out! We're not leaving! We're staying here!"

The minutes that followed were long. I spoke softly, trying to pacify her, but to no avail. She refused to answer or to come out. I have to admit that gave me a shock. But the very next morning, thanks to the extraordinary speed with which children adapt to changed circumstances, Alexandra came to me and said, "Don't worry, Daddy, it's going to be all right. I won't cry any more." As for Antoine, always the optimist, he didn't really mind the prospect of leaving Ottawa, especially as he and his sisters are very close to their cousins who are the same age and live in Montreal.

Still, the decision I had to make was difficult and heartrending. It meant I would have to leave my new M.P.s—people I had personally recruited: Elsie Wayne, who had so courageously shared the most difficult years; all the rank and file members of our party from one end of the country to the other who soldiered on, through the best and worst of times, steadfastly believing in the vision we proposed for the country; senators who had given me their help and advice when I most needed it; and, ultimately, it would mean leaving Parliament, a place where I had spent fourteen of the most eventful and rewarding years of my life. But in the end, after much soul-searching, I decided to answer the call.

The Challenges Facing Québec

The Quiet Revolution marked the beginning of an intensive period of modernization for Québec. During the last thirty years we saw the creation of new institutions that allowed us to forge a prominent cultural and economic role for ouselves in North American society. However, we must not become the victims of our own success. We cannot cling to the formulas that enabled us to reach this stage to the point where we lose all sense of judgement. The time has come to re-examine the solutions that worked for us in the past and ask ourselves whether they are still the right ones for the future. We must now look ahead to the next thirty years as those we will devote to the prosperity of our citizenry. We have done enough for the greater glory of the State.

From this point on all our energies must be directed toward enabling Québecers to enjoy the same standard of living as our neighbours throughout North America. It is an essential precondition to our being able to maintain our institutions, promote our language and build our communities. We have the benefit of a distinct language and culture that makes us unique and forms the foundation of our social solidarity. This distinctness is significant—the continuation of it facilitates Québec's success as a society. To ensure this success, Québec's political leaders must have their hands free. The Premier of Québec must not be constantly hampered by a political ideology that limits the choices he can make. To build Québec, we must first remove those blinders and recover the freedom to envisage our future without limits.

Autonomy through Solidarity

The most important role men and women can play is to rally the population around a number of key values and objectives. Leadership after all is not just the ability to understand and express reality as it is, but to go further and define our ultimate goals within the future we want to build. The challenge is not an easy one, for our destination lies beyond the horizon.

My mother and father felt we had to give to our lives meaning. I was taught to believe that our personal lives are intimately bound to those of the people around us. In my parents' eyes, individual success was important and desirable, but only had real meaning if your community was equally successful. It is with those memories and perspectives in mind that I approach political life.

The success of a society can be gauged by its ability to recognize the difficulties of the people around us. The true measure of our societal success is our capacity, in our search for solutions, to include the weak and vulnerable, i.e. the poor, the young, the aged and the sick. In doing so, we must avoid the trap of complacency. Each generation faces its own lot of problems and challenges. There is nothing to be gained from exaggerating them or wallowing in self-pity. What is needed instead is a lucid analysis of existing needs. We should set objectives based on those needs; then, mobilize our resources to ensure those objectives are met.

The Educational challenge

Education must be our number one priority. It needs to be seen in its true context: The information revolution and the demands of the new, knowledge-based economy pose new challenges for our educational system. Today and in the future, as never before, workers will need an educational background that equips them to deal with increasingly complex problems in an environment where constant, rapid change has become the norm.

Lifetime employment is no longer an option. Therefore, our educational system must ensure that our children receive a solid general education, one which will give them the flexibility to successfully deal with change. The knowledge revolution has brought with it technological progress, which, in turn, has coincided with the globalization of the free market economy and the free movement of capital and labour. This situation is actually a boon for our children, provided our educational system can adequately prepare them. A high-quality educational system, one which emphasizes success and provides a more effective transition between school and the job market, is the best guarantee of success for Québec in this new global environment.

My assessment of our income-support programs (Employment Insurance and Welfare) is a harsh one. Too often, these programs only confirm failure. They stigmatize, they marginalize. We have to change our government's outlook and approach to enable individuals in need to turn their lives around. That will mean rethinking these programs to reflect values like work, self-reliance and the need to contribute to society. More resources and more money must be made available. We must allow young people to participate in society and find their place within it by integrating them into the school system, vocational training programs, community work or by helping them enter the workforce.

In this regard we absolutely must avoid simplistic formulas. As soon as you mention the words *indivudual responsibility*, you are too often suspected of surreptitiously wanting to introduce a system that requires people to do forced labour in exchange for their welfare cheque. Nothing could be further from the truth. What is needed instead is a sustained, long-term effort by the whole of society—an effort to which everyone must contribute. This scenario means that the private sector, chambers of commerce and municipalities must stand up and take responsibility. It is in the interests of us all; each one of us must feel a responsibility toward all of our children.

No time to waste

Economically speaking, it is clear that the government initiatives of the past thirty years, though developed in good faith to solve problems, have multiplied to the point where they are now choking our economy. That is a universal conclusion that all governments, even the most left-of-center, have been forced to accept on the basis of the damage done to the public treasury. The saddest thing about it is the failure of leadership it reveals. In wanting to deal with specifics, leaders have lost sight of the general interest. In that, there is blame enough to go around. All political parties that formed governments in those years were guilty of the same excesses. The mistakes of the past hold lessons for the future.

But what is worse is allowing our social pendulum to swing to the other extreme, i.e. the recent, grim policies of the PQ regime. Having done nothing to remedy Québec's financial situation during its first year in power because it needed to finance its referendum strategy, the PQ leadership suddenly woke up to a problem that had grown much worse—and panicked. In their haste to change course, they smashed everything and made such a hash of the health care system that you sometimes wonder if they have not lost their heads. It has reached the shameful point where doctors are being forced to tell their patients, people who are sick and vulnerable, that their treatment has to be delayed or that the care they need, which is their right to expect, is not available. All this because the government is hell-bent on balancing the budget before a certain date in order to create the "winning conditions" for yet another referendum on secession.

It is unforgivable, not least because it is a hoax. The so-called zero deficit of Lucien Bouchard and Bernard Landry is really a deficit in disguise—a forgery, a fake. Since the 1995 referendum they have cynically forced hospitals and universities to rack up huge operating deficits ($500 million and $300 million respectively), not to mention CEGEPs (junior colleges) whose debt has increased by $100 million. Municipalities and school commissions have been respectively stuck by this government with $1.3 billion and $508 million worth of bills, thus imposing on them the odious task of reducing services and increasing the burden to taxpayers in order to be able to meet their budgets. When you add to that the PQ cuts to health care ($2.1 billion) and education ($1.4 billion), you realize that the zero that will appear as if by magic at the bottom of Bernard Landry's balance sheet in fact hides an appalling human deficit. On the economy, social services, health care, and education, the PQ regime has sacrificed the interests of the citizens of Québec to those of the PQ party and its ideology. At no time has the PQ regime concerned itself with the quality of public services.

Putting the state at the service of the citizen

The citizen must at last be placed at the center of the government's preoccupations. At the same time, the old interventionist State must become less omnipresent in our lives. The government must continue to protect the environment and public health, and promote education and training, but it should not intervene massively in the economy with risk capital and borrowed money as it does now. And the State should not be telling the regions of Québec how to develop their local economies. The mentality within the PQ regime is paternalistic and patronizing, unhealthy and counterproductive. People in the regions are perfectly capable of organizing and ensuring their own economic and social development. The State should assist that development, not stage-manage it. Economic growth in the regions will stop, or at least reduce, the outflow of young people from the regions toward major urban centers.

Like it or not, the backdrop for all our economic decisions is that we live in a North American economy where we compete with neighbours who are our competitors and pay less taxes than we do. In this regard, one of the most troubling symptoms of our economic problems in Québec is the brain-drain. In the last two years, in the critical area of health care, Montreal alone has lost 26 out of 243 orthopedists; 6 out 119 vascular surgeons, 12 out of 313 cardiologists; 4 out of 65 rheumatologists; and 5 out of 115 pathologists. These departures, however, represent only the tip of the iceberg. Countless families have lost children, some among the brightest of their generation, to greener pastures outside the province. In addition, the employment picture in some American states in certain critical economic sectors is particularly enticing: salaries are higher and taxes are lower. The cost of living is also much lower. When you are twenty four years old, you do not need a Ph.D. in economics to conclude that you can move elsewhere, earn more money and keep more of it in your pocket—an entirely legitimate ambition. Jobs and money make the economy go round. We should not see in that a contradiction with the need for social responsibility, quite to the contrary. A prosperous economy can afford to pay for more services to the population.

The demographic challenge

The State must return to its basic mission: education, health, and the integration of our economy into the wider North American environment. What is presently missing from the public debate is a recognition of demographic reality. Within the next fifteen years we will undergo demographic change unprecedented in our history. The consequence of that change will depend on our ability to prepare for it—now. Take my case: I am forty years old; in twenty-five years I will be sixty-five; one Québecer in four will then be sixty-five. This represents a formidable challenge for the future of our health care system, our old age pensions, the public debt, current taxpayers and those who will be footing the bill—our children. At the very least it seems obvious that it is in our own self-interest to make sure that the people of the younger generation are successful. We do not have the luxury of letting too many of them fall through the cracks. Time is running out.

We have about ten years ahead of us to make the right choices. In the meantime, the stakes must be properly explained to the electorate so we can make the right decisions today, decisions which will allow the government of Québec in fifteen, twenty or twenty-five years to offer the population the standard of living and quality of services it expects and deserves. We must be able to plan for these changes in a rational manner; not under the gun of a looming budget crisis. Policies that allow for sustained economic growth are therefore a necessity. We must accept that we live in the North American economy—the backdrop to all investment decisions.

Making the most of the Canadian partnership

One thing that really frustrates me is a mentality that says we should somehow be the servants of our political institutions. By that I mean the obsession with jurisdictional and constitutional structures. We are not born to be the servants of the Canadian Constitution, hampered in our outlook by constitutional structures. In a federation, where questions such as the economy, employment and the environment transcend jurisdictional boundaries, we must stop wasting time and energy on sterile debates. Instead, we should apply ourselves to setting concrete objectives and then making the federal system work to ensure that we meet those objectives. The Canadian employment insurance system, for example, has to be made flexible enough to be compatible, in its administration and programs, with the educational objectives we in Québec will set for ourselves.

We are no longer in the 1950's. The year 2000 will soon be upon us. For too long our leaders have behaved like children in a sandbox fighting over toys. This jockeying over jurisdiction has too often led to interminable arguments at the taxpayers' expense. It is not true that employment insurance, because it comes under federal jurisdiction, cannot be altered to be compatible with the education and training objectives set by the government of Québec. Let me be very clear: Employment insurance is a federal jurisdiction that must be put at the service of education and training objectives that will be set by Québecers. Québec can only gain from this. We will lose none of our influence within the federation, none of our powers as a province, and we will gain in terms of means. Here we are speaking of things that have a real impact on people's lives instead of on the outcome of the next symposium on the future of our federal institutions. Such an approach will obviously require a change in attitudes.

The challenge for Canada

We are entering a new era in Canada, one in which provincial governments have acquired a degree of autonomy they did not previously enjoy. This represents a considerable change. After the Second World War, Canadians wanted a number of social programs put in place—ones they still value very strongly. The federal government then had two advantages: First, it had the required financial capability to answer the call; second, it had a public service capable of designing and implementing programs, which was something the provincial administrations, other than Ontario and Québec, lacked. What has changed are the provincial governments, which have grown in size, competence and expertise. Today, they are better equipped than the federal government to design and deliver services to their populations. Now all we need to do is acknowledge these changes.

Some Canadians still believe the federal government alone can promote social programs. They are mistaken. They underestimate the common values that all Canadians deeply cherish. One aspect of our present federal system that needs to be corrected is the notion of accountability, which is not linked clearly enough to those making the decisions. Thus, the federal government in the last few years has gotten away with cutting transfers to the provinces without really being held accountable, which has only muddied the waters. We must ensure that accountability is clearly recognized, and that the responsibilities of each order of government are more clearly defined.

The objective I shall relentlessly pursue, in close collaboration with other Canadian political leaders, is the creation of mechanisms for co-management and co-decision in areas where both governments have a useful and complementary role to play. The federal government must recognize that provincial governments are now fully capable of discharging their responsibilities. This adjustment will require a more collegial form of federalism, one that reflects our common values and the fact that Canada is one of the oldest democracies in the world. Canada, under Baldwin and Lafontaine, was among the first nations to adopt ministerial responsibility. It is up to us to be the first to explore new forms of federalism and new ways of governing ourselves that are more in keeping with modern reality. This is where Québec's interests now lie.

Removing the referendum threat

Québec is faced with an additional obstacle—and a considerable one. This is the systematic blocking of any real progress due to the ideological blindness of an outdated regime that subordinates the true priorities of the citizens to its referendum objective. We are at a serious disadvantage in comparison with our neighbours because we are governed by people with no imagination who are interested only in settling century-old scores. Their vision of Québec's future is completely out of touch with reality. First: The secessionist objective with which they are obsessed runs counter to the wishes of a majority of Québecers. The majority of Québec voters, including francophones, feel a strong attachment to Canada and recognize the value of what we have built together. Second: The Québec sovereignist movement limits itself to blaming the rest of Canada for everything that, according to them, does not work in Québec. It is a movement that is bereft of any positive vision; to this day it has remained incapable of telling us what we would have to gain by seceding from Canada. Who would it benefit? And why?

We are now a matter of months or weeks away from a general election in Québec, in which we will again be asked to decide whether we want another referendum. Despite promises made by Lucien Bouchard after the last referendum to flesh out the "partnership" idea and explain what it would entail, we still do not know what it is about. The reason is quite simple: It is that we already have the partnership. Instead of striving to break it up, only to try and build a new one, in a crisis atmosphere, after negotiations, the outcome of which is utterly unpredictable, we should be funneling our energies into ensuring that what we have works properly. As long as we allow ourselves to be governed by these people from another era, all the energy we should be devoting to building our economy and pursuing a broader ideal will be wasted and lost. While the Parizeau government was busy inventing all sorts of structures to spread its sovereignist propaganda among the population, no one was looking after the real problems of the citizenry. Even as entire teams of senior civil servants were readied to manage the economic aftershocks of a YES vote, or to decide where, in the future capital of an independent Québec the foreign embassies would be built, the task of putting Québec's fiscal house in order was put on hold for fear of antagonizing voters on the eve of a referendum. While Lucien Bouchard continues to busy himself with inflicting on Québecers the so-called "winning conditions" for his projected referendum, Québec will continue to divide and weaken itself. To the existing political uncertainty he adds only confusion and ambiguity. What would these winning conditions be? No one is telling us. And our future, because of it, is doubly uncertain.

In order for Québec to succeed, the Québec government must be willing to operate in the Canadian and North American milieu. This will require a change in attitude on our part in favour of firmness and cooperation. When Lucien Bouchard meets with the other provincial premiers he can pretend to take part in their discussions when it suits his own electoral purposes, which he did at a recent meeting in Saskatoon. But everyone knows he isn't serious about improving the federation. As Premier, I want to be able to speak forcefully when the circumstances require it. I don't want to be suspected of resorting to provocation aimed at validating my secessionist credo in the eyes of the voters back home. The

Premier of Québec must be completely free to express and implement the mandates given to him by Québecers. He cannot have his partners doubting his good faith at every turn. Growth and prosperity are the challenges we face.

The presence of a PQ regime in Québec City has another perverse effect: It lets the federal government think it can get away with anything. As soon as there is a disagreement, knowing that the avowed objective of their Québec counterpart is to break up the federation rather than improve it, the federal government has a perfect excuse to stonewall and do nothing. However, the federal government will not so easily duck the issues once it is faced with a Liberal government in Québec. Discussions between us are going to be frank. We are finally going to be able to enjoy mature political debates in Canada without the very existence of our country being put into question every time a disagreement arises. On that score, let us harbour no illusions. There will be disagreements, and there is nothing wrong with that. The day we all start thinking alike is the day I start to worry. This is Canada, after all, not the former Soviet Union.

Time to get out of the ruts of the past

What is absurd about the sovereignist side of the current debate on national unity, and what is disturbing, is the way our entire history and our future, are reduced to a constant rehashing of past episodes of our constitutional negotiations. The patriation of the Canadian Constitution in 1982 did not happen the way it should have. It was the failure of the men and women of that generation of politicians. We also have to accept that the Meech Lake failure was not a failure of Canada or Québec—it was the failure of the men and women who, in good faith, at that particular moment in history, proposed the Accord. It didn't work. So, let's stop pointing fingers and leave that failure where it belongs—in the past.

We must understand our history in terms of the very foundations of the country we have built here in Canada. Francophones had the wisdom, right from the start, to realize that our community, language and culture would not long survive in North America if we did not reach an understanding with the British when they took possession of the continent after the French abandoned it through the Treaty of Paris. The British also had the wisdom to understand they had no hope of preserving their North American possessions, given the ambitions of the Americans, unless they reached an agreement with the 60,000 French-speakers who lived in this corner of the continent. Today, just in Québec, francophones are more than six and a half million strong, seven and a half million when you count francophones in other provinces. That is one quarter of Canada's population. And the sovereignists argue that we should give it all up by seceding from Canada. What nonsense.

The Canadian partnership has served us well. Our collective genius as Canadians has been to extend and expand it, first by going beyond the limits imposed by the Act of Union, then by the Act of Confederation, which created four provinces and a federal government. The federation grew as other provinces joined in. By 1999 it will include ten provincial governments and three territorial governments in addition to the government of Canada. At each stage of our history, with each new generation of leaders, this political partnership has evolved to become a social and economic partnership based on common values. We must continue to build that partnership. It must include Aboriginal peoples who until now have been excluded. We are not alone in facing the challenge of building a new relationship with Aboriginal peoples. The countries of Latin America, Mexico, the United States, New Zealand and Australia all face the same challenge. It is one of the major issues confronting us in the coming century, and one that will test our societal values. In Québec we face the added challenge of reaching out to Western Canadians, whose concerns we must understand and address.

Rebuilding the bridges

Our future depends on our capacity to come to terms with our identity. One major challenge for Canada as a whole will be its ability to see that our Constitution reflects who we are so we can recognize ourselves in the document that describes us. A Constitution is a society's mirror. And Québec's image is reflected in that mirror. But in that image, as in the image of the Aboriginal peoples of this country, something is missing from the total picture. For Québecers the advantage of the distinct society clause in the Meech Lake Accord, something not adequately understood elsewhere, was that it would have served as a bridge. It was a way of formally expressing the Québécois identity within the framework of our Canadian citizenship. When the bridge came crashing down, the shock wave had a brutal impact on the tone and substance of political debate in this country. But the solution is not to give up and turn inward. The solution is to learn from past mistakes and build a better, stronger bridge, taking into account the topography on both sides of the river.

We have to find a better way of expressing who we are. That being said, we will not ask for permission to be ourselves. We must not fall into the trap of believing that we can substitute political structures for our common political will, that of Québecers and all Canadians, to go on living together and sharing a common destiny. A Constitution must express our will and not take its place. Beyond language, culture and territory, a country is defined by a common history, common experiences, common values, and a constantly renewed will to live together. That will cannot be legislated. It has to be felt. That common will exists today. It reflects our values, those which allow us to live in a country that is different from all others. The country we have created could not exist without Québec. The time has come to resume the too long interrupted work of building with our partners. Québec can no longer afford to stand apart from the North American economy and the changes underway within the federation that affect our interests. We must instead participate actively and constructively so the decisions that are made reflect our needs and the objectives we will set for ourselves. We must do this for the greater good of Québecers and all Canadians, now and in the future.

Why I Came Home

My family and I will soon be leaving North Hatley to move into our new home in Montreal. The last weeks have been chaotic. We have had four addresses in as many months. The moves required some adjustment. We spent the month of July here in the Eastern Townships. The children were reunited with their cousins and their friends in the village. Amélie is now fifteen. She is already telling us about the trips she is planning, the studies she wants to undertake, and the day when she and her cousin will share an apartment—it is a trying time in the life of a father. Antoine, at ten, is at that wonderful age when boys worship their mothers. He is curious, funny, full of projects and, for the time being, a bit more interested in his computer than his homework. Alexandra, our youngest, is only eight, but she is not afraid to assert herself. She, too, is full of enthusiasm for the future and looks forward to the day when she will be... ten! As for Michou, through all the upheavals of the last few months, she has, once again, with extraordinary steadfastness and love, accepted to share my choices. We have just spent precious time together with our children and with our respective families before embarking upon a course that will be both challenging and demanding.

I took advantage of these few weeks' vacation to assemble several working groups, made up of experts and collaborators from across the province, to refine my positions and develop my knowledge of Québec issues. Accepting to lead a party does not mean you know all the answers in advance. You have to get informed. You must learn and prepare. You have to debate the options the Québec government is facing in health, education, tax policy, etc. with a view to ensuring sustained economic growth. So we applied ourselves to preparing for the Fall session of the National Assembly. In the area of health care alone, the failure of the PQ regime is overwhelming. After the election, we have an obligation to be prepared to act as rapidly as possible to restore the health services to which all citizens in the province are entitled. We do not have the right to make empty promises. Our commitments will be firm and clear. Above all, we want to be able to implement them as quickly possible.

These few weeks of calm have made it possible for me to write this book, which is not as complete as it might have been had I not run out of time. In particular, it does not do justice to all those who accompanied me during my fifteen years in federal politics. Those who, each in his or her own way, devoted themselves to assisting me and supporting me. They know what I owe them, and so do I. However, before closing, I would like to summarize in a few words the future I envision for us, our society and for our children.

Last spring I had a decision to make. I came home to Québec because I am a Québecer. I was born here; my roots are here; this is where I have always lived. I chose Québec because I am forty years old and I cannot bear the fact that we have been going around in circles for as long as I can remember. The time has come to free ourselves from old dogmas, old ways of thinking and old antagonisms that are stifling Québec's progress.

I came home because I believe I can play a useful role in helping my fellow Québecers prosper and reach their true potential. I decided to join all of those who, like me, have great ambitions for Québec, ambitions that transcend the debate that has preoccupied us for the last twenty years. Our interests are not presently well served. We have a government that continues to place its secessionist imperative above the true interests of citizens. It divides the population, wastes our energies and our money in the pursuit of an objective that a majority of Québecers have rejected twice in fifteen years. The time has come to turn the page and get to work at collectively building a truly great country. We can do much better than we are doing at the moment. When I listen to the speeches of Lucien Bouchard or Bernard Landry, who declare themselves satisfied and even congratulate themselves for the current situation, I cannot believe my ears. It just cannot be. They do not see what is going on all around us. One statistic alone tells us everything we need to know: Québec, in the last twenty years, lost over four hundred thousand people. This betrays a deep malaise. Four hundred thousand people is more than the population of Laval, the second largest city in Québec. All those people have pulled up stakes and left. There is a reason for that. It is the worst thing that can happen to an economy. An economy that works is an economy that attracts people. What is happening here is the opposite. Montreal is a city that has been emptying for years; one that has become poorer, and it is the very symbol of the failure of the PQ regime.

I came home because I want to offer new solutions to our problems; I am tired of seeing us divided; I want to see us united; I want our children to want to stay here and continue to build their dreams. We need a second Quiet Revolution—one that will put the State at the service of the citizens. Restoring hope means we must once again start building on foundations that are stable, without blinders and without restrictions. Our ancestors did not wait for constitutional changes to build our country. We have no right to diminish the inheritance we will leave to our children. History once again beckons us to a great endeavour; to a collective effort worthy of all those who came before us. Let us roll up our sleeves and get to work.

Jean Charest
North Hatley, July-August 1998

Table of Contents

 PRINTED IN CANADA